Routledge Revivals

The Gold Standard and Its Future

First published in 1931, *The Gold Standard and Its Future* by T.E. Gregory offers a detailed analysis of the gold standard's mechanics, its recent history, and its breakdown in Great Britain and the U.S.A. The book examines the causes and consequences of these disruptions through theoretical and statistical perspectives, explores official literature on the subject, and provides a personal interpretation of the gold standard's future. A vital resource for understanding monetary history and policy.

The Gold Standard and Its Future

T. E. Gregory

Routledge
Taylor & Francis Group
Routledge Revivals

First published in 1931
by Methuen

This edition first published in 2026 by Routledge
4 Park Square, Milton Park, Abingdon, Oxon, OX14 4RN

and by Routledge
605 Third Avenue, New York, NY 10158

Routledge is an imprint of the Taylor & Francis Group, an informa business

Publisher's Note
The publisher has gone to great lengths to ensure the quality of this reprint but points out that some imperfections in the original copies may be apparent.

Disclaimer
The publisher has made every effort to trace copyright holders and welcomes correspondence from those they have been unable to contact.

For Product Safety Concerns and Information please contact our EU representative GPSR@taylorandfrancis.com. Taylor & Francis Verlag GmbH, Kaufingerstraße 24, 80331 München, Germany

A Library of Congress record exists under LCCN: 32010808

ISBN: 978-1-041-30045-8 (hbk)
ISBN: 978-1-003-77260-6 (ebk)
ISBN: 978-1-041-30049-6 (pbk)

Book DOI 10.4324/9781003772606

THE GOLD STANDARD AND ITS FUTURE

by

T. E. GREGORY
SIR E. CASSEL PROFESSOR OF ECONOMICS IN THE UNIVERSITY OF LONDON

THIRD EDITION
REVISED AND ENLARGED

METHUEN & CO. LTD. *LONDON*
36 Essex Street Strand

First Published	*December 23rd 1931*
Second Edition (with new Introduction)	*November 1932*
Third Edition (revised and rewritten) .	*1934*
First American Edition . . .	*1932*
First Japanese Edition . . .	*1934*

PRINTED IN GREAT BRITAIN

FROM THE PREFACE TO THE FIRST EDITION

THE QUESTION whether or not Great Britain should return to the gold standard must necessarily dominate any discussions of the gold problem in this country for some time to come. While I hope that I have never lost sight of this, to us, fundamental issue, I have tried, in my treatment of the whole gold problem, to give concrete expression to my belief that the part which gold is called upon to play in the creation of an integrated price and income structure has received too little attention in recent discussion. For that there are several reasons, one of them being that it is not easy to bring out clearly yet simply the full significance of the mechanism by which this integration is achieved and the complex character of the conditions in which, and in which alone, the gold standard mechanism can function satisfactorily. It is for others to say how far the present attempt has been successful. While I hope that I have not been in any way neglectful of fact, this book is not primarily intended to be a chronicle of recent events, but an attempt at an analysis of fundamental conditions. . . .

I desire to express my great indebtedness to the help afforded me at every stage of the progress of this book by Mrs. Annette Henderson, B.Sc.(Econ.). To Professor Lionel Robbins I am obliged for critical discussion of a difficult point of analysis.

T. E. GREGORY

THE LONDON SCHOOL OF ECONOMICS
AND POLITICAL SCIENCE
November 9th 1931

FROM THE PREFACE TO THE SECOND EDITION

APART FROM a few verbal corrections, I have left the text of this book unchanged, preferring to bring the subject-matter up-to-date, in so far as that was necessary, by means of a new Introduction. . . .

T. E. GREGORY

THE LONDON SCHOOL OF ECONOMICS
AND POLITICAL SCIENCE
July 12th 1932

PREFACE TO THE THIRD EDITION

THIS BOOK was originally written almost immediately after the suspension of the gold standard in Great Britain, and its general tone was, of course, profoundly influenced by that event, the full consequences of which could not be foreseen at the time. Now that a new edition is called for, substantial alterations appear necessary: readers who compare this edition with its predecessors will find that the second half of the book is new and that two additional chapters have been required to deal with the march of events in the U.S.A. and with the course of international discussion: whilst the chapters on Great Britain and on the future of the gold standard have been very largely rewritten. In its new form, therefore, this book is both longer and covers a wider range of considerations than it did before. I hope that in its new form it may continue to commend itself to students of the subject.

I have again to express my deep indebtedness to Mrs. A. Henderson, B.Sc.(Econ.). She alone is responsible for the charts and for the revision of the Statistical Appendix, and I am further under obligation to her for general assistance without which the completion of the book would have been greatly delayed.

T. E. GREGORY

THE LONDON SCHOOL OF ECONOMICS
AND POLITICAL SCIENCE
August 21st 1934

CONTENTS

STATISTICAL APPENDIX

'BESIDES WHICH,' continued Mr. Gregsbury, 'I should expect him now and then to go through a few figures in the printed tables, and to pick out a few results, so that I might come out pretty well on timber-duty questions, and finance questions, and so on: and I should like him to get up a few little arguments about the disastrous effects of a return to cash payments and a metallic currency, with a touch now and then about the exportation of bullion, and the Emperor of Russia and bank notes and all that kind of thing, which it's only necessary to talk fluently about, because nobody understands it. Do you take me?'

'I think I understand,' said Nicholas.

Nicholas Nickleby, Chap. XVI

THE GOLD STANDARD
AND ITS FUTURE

CHAPTER I

THE GENERAL NATURE OF THE GOLD STANDARD AND THE PROBLEM OF INTERNATIONAL EQUILIBRIUM

THE INTERNATIONAL gold standard is essentially a creation of the second half of the nineteenth century. At the end of the Napoleonic Wars the currency systems of the world, with very few exceptions (Great Britain being by far the most important), were based either upon silver as the sole foundation of the system or upon silver in combination with gold. Between 1848, when gold was discovered in hitherto unknown quantities in Australia and California, and 1914, when the disaster of the World War inaugurated a revolutionary change in the monetary situation, there occurred a gradual but, in the end, an almost universal transition from these silver or mixed currency systems to gold. Between 1919 and 1925 a co-operative and successful effort was made to replace the monetary systems of the world upon a firm foundation, and the international gold standard was thereby restored. In the last few years a variety of circumstances have combined to imperil this work of restoration. The collapse of the gold standard in a number of raw material producing countries in the course of 1930 was followed by the suspension of the gold standard in a number of European countries in 1931. The most important country to be driven off was Great Britain, which had reverted to gold after the War by the Gold Standard Act of April 1925. The Gold Standard (Amendment) Act, passed on September 25th 1931, by suspending the gold standard in this country, led not only to suspension by the Scandinavian countries and by Finland, but also to suspension in Ireland and India. Other countries followed, including Japan and the U.S.A. The purpose of this book is to discuss the issues raised in consequence of these events. These issues are contained in the answers to the following questions: Ought the international gold standard to be restored? Ought Great Britain herself to return to the gold standard? Under what conditions should Great Britain return to gold? The more important of these questions is the second one. Just as Great Britain's departure from gold necessitated a number of other countries suspending the gold standard, so a return to gold by Great Britain would be an important factor in deciding these others to return to gold also. A refusal by Great Britain to return to gold would, in any event, be a fact of major importance, even if her example were not followed by other countries, as, indeed, it might be. For the world has hitherto, except in periods of grave dislocation, regarded a common, i.e. a truly international standard, as a *sine qua non* of normal and orderly economic progress; and Great Britain has played an extraordinarily important part in the evolution of the modern world and in creating the prestige of the gold standard. If Great Britain were permanently to depart from the group of gold standard countries, the significance of the international gold standard would change profoundly, and the consequences to the countries still remaining upon the gold standard, as well as to Great Britain herself, would be, whether on balance good or evil, of the highest importance.

These various issues will become clearer as the analysis proceeds. The first step to an understanding of the present situation must consist in appreciating the relationship between gold and the monetary institutions of the modern world.

Economic society is built up upon the basis of a few exceedingly important but simple principles: the division of labour, the existence of private property, and free exchange. These principles are incapable of being reconciled with one another without the presence, at the same time, in every economic community, of some unit of account in which relative values can be expressed. This is true, even if no such thing as money, i.e. a medium of exchange, actually passed from hand to hand in exchange for commodities and services rendered, had come into existence. The reason is obvious on reflection. With every increase in the number of separate transactions taking place, the difficulties of pure barter would increase. In fact, the difficulties would be such that the mere existence of barter would effectively *prevent* the development of exchange, and, with it, the possibility of extending the subdivision of processes of production and thus the growth of economic well-being. It is only when all the rates of exchange between commodities and services, not only exchange between goods here and now, but between goods here and now for goods in the future, are capable of being expressed in one common symbol that prices (i.e. relative values) become comparable. The first requisite, then, of a society organized for exchange is the existence of such a symbol or unit of account. But, in order to facilitate, not only comparison of the relative values of commodities and services, but also their exchange, it is necessary to provide, as well as a symbol or unit of account, a representative of that unit, or of its subdivisions and multiples, which can be passed from hand to hand and is freely acceptable in exchange for all the goods being offered on the market. Thus a community requires both a unit of account and a medium of exchange. Prices are *expressed* in terms of the unit of account, the British unit being the pound sterling, but commodities and services are exchanged for *money*. The price of a thing at any moment is determined by the quantity of money which has to be given for it, but the 'quantity of money' is a magnitude which is, in part, determined by the nature of the unit of account employed. The length of a sentence depends on the number of words in it, but the number of words itself depends upon the particular language which is employed. It follows from all this that the 'price level' is a highly elaborate concept: since its *meaning* turns upon the particular monetary language (units of account) and the particular money in which it is expressed.

Obviously, the important point for consideration now is the relationship between the thing or things which are called generically 'money' and the unit of account, which is, after all, only the language for the expression of monetary *magnitudes*. Consider the significance of the name of the British unit of account—the pound. This suggests a *weight*, and, indeed, the British pound sterling was originally a troy pound of *silver*. So long as the 'pound' remained a pound troy weight of silver, the unit of account was a real *thing*, as well as being the language in which currency magnitudes were expressed; and the relationship between the money and the unit of account was, at the same time, the relationship between one quantity of metal and another, provided that the coins all continued to be made of the substance of which the unit of account represented a certain weight. If the 'pound' for monetary purposes was divided into twenty shillings and two hundred and forty pence, all of them made of silver, and the 'silver pound' was a pound troy weight of silver, then a shilling represented one-twentieth and the penny one two-hundred-and-fortieth part, by *weight*, of a pound weight of silver. (What quantity of silver a pound weight of it is, is itself a separate problem, but that cannot be considered here.) The whole difficulty in understanding modern currency systems arises from the fact that we have departed from the sweet simplicity of earlier days. The language remains largely the same but the meaning has altered, just as language has altered its meaning in other connections also.

In the first place, the intimate connection between money and the unit of account, which existed so long as the unit of account did stand for a defined weight of *something*, and the coins or 'money' were all made of the same metal, so that each represented physically a defined quantity of metal determined by its arithmetical relation to the unit of account, became weakened. Certain coins acquired a face value greater than their metallic content, and coins having a certain arithmetical relation to the unit of account were made of a material different from that represented by the unit of account. In either or both of these ways, though the unit of account might continue to represent a certain weight of metal, the metal to which in the end the whole currency system was related ceased to play the same role as previously in the actual composition of the coinage. In fact, the coinage itself began to play a subordinate role. The actual media by which transactions were settled, and are settled in the modern world, are overwhelmingly non-metallic. They consist of bank notes and of bank deposits subject to cheque. The whole mass of purchasing power retains only this connection with the physical thing with which the unit of account is associated—that each and every form of purchasing power, bronze and copper, silver, bank notes and bank deposits, is ultimately convertible into the physical substance of which the unit of account represents a certain weight. If that physical substance is gold, the whole mass of purchasing power is convertible into gold, so long as the unit of account represents a certain weight of gold and *so long as convertibility is effectively sustained.* It does not matter if some forms of purchasing power are not directly convertible into gold so long as each individual form of purchasing power is convertible into a form which is so convertible. If bank deposits are convertible into Bank of England notes and Bank of England notes are effectively convertible into gold, the mass of British purchasing power is linked to gold and Great Britain is upon the gold standard; for all forms of purchasing power in Great Britain are expressed in terms of pounds sterling. So long as the pound sterling stands for a certain and defined weight of gold and so long as that weight of gold can be obtained freely in exchange for a pound, or, what is the same thing, so long as a certain quantity of gold can be obtained in exchange for the number of British pounds which, under existing legislation, represents that quantity of gold, the exchange value of British pounds in terms of gold cannot fall below that fixed by law. In addition, if, in exchange for a certain weight of gold representing a certain number of British pounds, that number of pounds sterling can always be obtained, the value of British currency, again in terms of gold, cannot rise above the relationship fixed by law. To put the matter concretely, so long as the Bank of England is by law obliged to buy gold at the rate of £3 17*s.* 9*d.* per standard ounce (containing 11 parts gold out of 12) and is obliged by law to sell gold in exchange for its notes at the rate of £3 17*s.* 10½*d.* per standard ounce, an ounce of standard gold cannot be worth less or more, in terms of English money, than £3 17*s.* 9*d.* or £3 17*s.* 10½*d.* respectively. Or, what is again the same thing, since £3 17*s.* 9*d.* = 1,866 halfpence and £3 17*s.* 10½*d.* = 1,869 halfpence and £1 = 480 halfpence, the value of a British pound, so long as effective convertibility is maintained, cannot move outside the limits of $\frac{480}{1866}$ and $\frac{480}{1869}$ parts of an ounce troy of standard gold.

The second point to be borne in mind, however, is that this connection between the unit of account and a certain weight of metal need *not* be maintained. Effective convertibility may be suspended, as it was by the Gold Standard (Amendment) Act on September 25th 1931. In that case the unit of account ceases to have any definite relationship to a defined weight of gold, and becomes purely a symbol. Whether a piece of paper called a pound or a bank deposit of one pound convertible into a pound note will continue to possess the same purchasing power in terms of gold, i.e. will buy as much gold as it did before, or more of it or less of it, now becomes a matter of doubt. The essential fact about the gold standard is that it guarantees a currency system a fixed gold value, that is, a value which cannot change so long as convertibility is effective and the gold weight of the unit of account has not been changed. The essential fact about a currency which is *not* upon the gold standard is that its gold value is *indeterminate*. Whether it is better to have a currency system with a determinate or indeterminate gold value is the fundamental essential issue which flows from our recent departure from a fixed relationship.

When a whole series of countries possess currency systems which have a fixed relationship with gold of the kind described above, an international gold standard system comes into existence, not in any formal fashion, but as a matter of fact. The only intelligible meaning to be assigned to the phrase 'the international gold standard' is the simultaneous presence, in a group of countries, of arrangements by which, in each of them, gold is convertible at a fixed rate into the local currency and the local currency into gold, and by which gold movements from any one of these areas to any of the others are freely permitted by all of them. In these circumstances, but only in these, are the following consequences possible.

First, each such currency will have at any moment of time fixed limits of value in terms of the others; and these limits of value will vary from time to time according to the cost of moving gold from centre to centre. If by law £1 sterling is equivalent to 113 grains, by weight, of fine gold and if this amount of gold obtains, and is obtained for, £1 sterling whilst, at the same time, $4·866$\dot{6}$ American also and at all times obtains and is obtained for 113 grains of fine gold, then the value of £1 in terms of dollars cannot be worth *less* in terms of dollars than $4·866$\dot{6}$ *minus* the cost of shipping 113 grains of gold from London to New York, or worth more in terms of dollars than $4·866$\dot{6}$, *plus* the cost of shipping 113 grains of gold from New York to London. If pounds were worth more or less than this in terms of dollars, or dollars less or more than this in terms of pounds, gold *would* move, so long as the gold could be obtained. It is true that in moments of panic two currencies both nominally and actually upon the gold standard can and have, in fact, exchanged at rates outside the limits set by the cost of gold shipments (the so-called 'gold points'). But that is due to very exceptional circumstances; the amount of gold capable of being sent within a given time is limited by the shipment and insurance facilities available; moral pressure may have been applied to *prevent* gold shipments or, at least, rumours to that effect may be circulating and panic-stricken individuals, rather than wait their turn or, perhaps, fearing that their turn will never come, prefer to buy at a loss, hoping thereby to avoid still bigger losses in the future.

From the standpoint of business and commerce, the great advantage of the international gold standard is precisely that, whilst it is in working order, *it eliminates fluctuating rates of exchange.* The degree to which, within the gold points, rates of exchange can vary is so limited that, provided there is certainty that the system will continue, international trade and investment can be conducted without any fear that the sums risked in a particular trade or investment transaction will not be recovered, or will only be partly recovered, owing to changes in the relative exchange values of different moneys at the date of payment. It is true that, if the whole world, or a great part of it, were to link its currency systems to one particular currency, the advantages of fixity of exchange could be attained, even if that one currency were not itself linked to gold. On the other hand, other possible advantages of being upon the gold standard might have to be sacrificed. It is also true that if, in the absence of an international gold standard or in the absence of any arrangement for linking up all currencies with a single one of them (say sterling), the market in 'forward exchange' were functioning perfectly, the risks of exchange to the individual could be avoided, at any rate for the greater part, though not without additional expense. If, e.g., all rights to receive *future* payments in any currency could be sold at a fixed price in advance or all obligations to pay in the future could be covered in advance, through sales and purchases in the 'forward exchange' market, the risks attaching to the dissociation of currencies from a firm gold substratum would be diminished. But the fact appears to be that, just when the relative values of currencies are most uncertain and when, therefore, the advantages to be derived from the organization of a forward exchange market would be greatest, the difficulties of organizing it, in all currencies and for all maturities, i.e. dates in advance, are greatest also. The future market in exchange, if perfect, would eliminate exchange risks, though at a price. But it appears to be very difficult in practice to organize a perfect market except when currencies are not likely to fluctuate much, and that is just when such a market is least needed. There can be no question that the development of an international gold standard in the second half of the nineteenth century and the enormous growth of international trade and investment which then took place are no mere coincidences. The development of the one implied the development of the other. Since the new countries then being opened up required enormous masses of capital for development purposes and because such capital could only be obtained if the lenders were reasonably certain of the value of principal and interest, the debtor nations were obliged to go on to the gold standard; the gold standard in its turn facilitated further loans and investments and at the same time made international trade a very much simpler operation. The international gold standard was thus, historically, one of the most important adjuncts to the opening up of the world to settlement and exploitation, and, whatever may be said by those who never look at the wood because of the trees, this *creation of a world economy* constitutes one of the great (and beneficial) turning-points in the history of mankind.

From the standpoint of the economist, however, there is another aspect of the situation which necessarily plays a large part in theoretical discussions relating to the significance of an international gold standard. This is the part played by gold movements in the establishment of the conditions necessary to secure equilibrium in the international balances of payment of the various countries upon the gold standard. An understanding of this matter is necessary in order that the method of adjusting the international balances of payment when countries are *not* upon the gold standard can be contrasted with the mechanism of gold standard adjustments, so that the advantages and disadvantages of the two alternative processes can be properly weighed.

The argument will be conducted in stages. First, it is assumed that there is an isolated community in which there circulates only a currency composed entirely of metallic coins. Assume further a given population with a certain average degree of efficiency. *The quantity of money* in this community will obviously depend upon the output of the mines (less the proportion of the output which is consumed directly in the form of ornament and hoards) and the number of coin units which under the prevailing conditions can be made out of a certain weight of metal. *The aggregate money income* of the community (i.e. the receipts of all the producers) will depend upon the current output of goods (which depends upon efficiency) multiplied by their prices. But what determines the prices of the output? In the case under consideration the supply of *new* money represents the net income of the gold producers: the goods they buy bring in an additional income to those who produce them and they are in their turn in a position to buy more. Hence prices will rise in the process of distributing the new supplies of money, and, given the output of the community, the greater the supply of new money the higher the price level will tend to be, over time. If for any reason, say a change in average efficiency, the output of goods increases, the price level, given a certain supply of purchasing power, may fall but money incomes may remain the same or even increase; for the tendency of falling prices of products to cause money incomes to fall may be more than offset by the increase in aggregate productivity.

Suppose now that this isolated community establishes trading relations with a second community with a lower level of prices and a lower range of money incomes. Trade will take the form of an export of metal from the first community to the second and an export of goods from the second community to the first. The 'balance of payments' will be adjusted entirely by an export of metal from the first community to begin with. But the effect of such an export of metal must be that the supply of money will diminish in that community and will increase in the second. The prices of the goods formerly demanded by the gold-miners of the first community will begin to fall and the money incomes of the producers of such goods will also fall. As the effects begin to be diffused among all the producers, both prices and money incomes begin generally to decline. The opposite process will take place in the metal importing community: the money incomes of those who export commodities will rise and, by increasing their monetary purchasing power, the imports of metal will enable prices and money incomes generally to rise. How long can this process go on? Until the general level of prices and the general level of money incomes in the two communities are the same? If the two communities were in all respects similar this might be conceivable, but in that case, as soon as prices and money incomes were on a level of equality, all trade would cease until, by a fresh increase in the supplies of metal in the metal producing community, prices were in disequilibrium again. The matter is obviously more complicated than this.

Communities do not, in fact, produce all commodities

equally efficiently. Whatever the general level of prices in a community may be, some goods will be lower in price than others, because these goods are produced either with more than average efficiency or because their producers are obliged, in consequence of peculiarities of their situation, to accept unusually low returns for their products. If, then, two communities enter into trading relations, each will export to the other those of its goods which are cheaper in the exporting than in the importing area. The mere fact that the general level of money incomes is higher in one community or that the general range of prices is higher there will not necessarily invalidate the point that *some* commodities may be cheaper. But suppose that for some reason there is an excess of imports over exports in the case of one of the two trading areas. The other area will then have an excess of exports over imports. Gold will flow (if the monetary metal is gold) into the country with the excess of exports. Again, this will affect

(*a*) Prices and, through prices,
(*b*) Money incomes in both areas.

In the gold exporting area prices and incomes will fall, and they will rise in the gold importing area. At the new level of prices in the gold exporting area a new range of goods becomes exportable; and, since prices are rising in the gold importing area, a certain range of goods now becomes less exportable than previously. But this is tantamount to saying that, given this new situation, exports will rise in the first case and fall in the second, until in fact they are adjusted to one another in aggregate value; for, until they are, gold will continue to move. An adjusted or equilibrated position of the balance of payments comes about when the relative position of prices and money incomes in the two countries becomes such that no metal need move from one to the other and, in the absence of disturbing causes, free gold movements will *force* this adjusted or equilibrated condition to come about.

But such an adjusted position does *not* require all prices and the general level of money incomes to be the same in both areas. On the contrary, the country with the greater efficiency will tend to have the lower level of prices and the higher range of money incomes. The reason for this is clear: since a unit of goods will be produced there more cheaply, *on the average*, it will tend to have a favourable export surplus and will attract gold to it in proportion to its efficiency. It is not the case that the international gold standard implies an identical *price level* (except as regards goods which are internationally traded and then transport costs must be considered), still less an identical range of money incomes. What the international gold standard does do is to force prices and money incomes in different trading areas into such a relationship that the balance of payments can be adjusted without gold flows in either direction. To put the matter somewhat differently, the international gold standard creates, *not a common price level but an integrated price and income structure*, the various parts of which stand in an organic relationship to one another.

These truths remain fundamentally the same when allowances are made for the complexities of modern currency systems, for the existence of tariffs and of transactions other than the direct exchange of present goods for present goods, i.e. for capital and interest transactions and for such extra-economic payments as tribute or reparations. But an important proviso is necessary at this place. In spite of the existence of complicated currency systems, tariffs, capital and interest transactions and reparations transfers, the international gold standard will produce equilibrium *if it is allowed to do so.* The dissatisfaction with the working of the gold standard in recent years, a dissatisfaction the grounds for which will be examined more closely in the next chapter, is due in the main to the fact that the implicit logic of that international standard has not always been clearly grasped and that it has not been *allowed* to function in the manner in which, if other views had prevailed, it would have done. The general conditions in which, with all the complications mentioned above, the international gold standard would produce equilibrium may be indicated here.

(1) The price and income structure of a modern economic community is *in the first instance* determined by the operations of the organized banking system, in the end by the credit policy of the Central Bank which, upon the basis of a given gold stock or reserve, can build up a given volume of notes and deposits, serving as the reserves of the commercial banks. If the community is to remain upon the gold standard, the task of the Central Bank amounts to controlling the effective volume of purchasing power in such a way that its aggregate amount does not exceed the amount dictated by the necessities of international equilibrium. If it does not do so it loses its gold. A number of possibilities exist. Equilibrium will be restored if, in the outside world, the price and income structure moves upwards; the task of the local Central Bank in that case is to prevent an upward movement at home until equilibrium is restored. The Central Bank may attempt to lower the level of local prices and incomes. Alternatively, an attempt may be made, by means of an increase in the efficiency of production, to lower the level of selling prices *without* a lowering of the level of money incomes. *Any* of these

three alternatives would produce effective equilibrium in the sense that gold flows cease and the balance of payments is adjusted solely by the movement of goods and services; and, moreover, there is no reason to suppose that the real magnitude of the underlying transactions should be less than it was before. But none of these solutions is necessary, in the sense that they are the only ones which are practically conceivable, though one or other of them is necessary in order to produce stable equilibrium. Two other alternatives are practically conceivable which would *not* produce stable equilibrium in the above sense. First, in order to stop the gold flow, the Central Bank may borrow an amount equal to the *current* deficit on the balance of payments. This will stop the gold flow but will not stop the causes of the flow unless other things happen as well. Next, the attempt to alter the income and price structure may fail, but the gold flow may be brought to an end by a more devious route. The price level being relatively too high, exports are checked, and this creates unemployment in the exporting industries. The aggregate volume of the national income therefore falls and consequently reduces both the demand for foreign products and the possibilities of savings. But it is not likely—the price structure being what it is—that the demand for foreign goods will fall off in proportion. In absolute magnitude it may even increase, though it will not increase as much as it would have done if unemployment had not prevailed. The adjustment may come through the falling off in the volume of savings reducing the quantity of effective new saving which can be made. If there is accruing an income from past investments from foreign countries, the adjustment may take the form of this income being used to meet the excess of imports at the expense of additional savings in the future. There is no *a priori* guarantee that the demand for foreign goods will confine itself to the limits within which it remains possible to finance imports by the utilization of income from abroad: and then gold losses of a cumulative kind may make themselves manifest. But, even if they do, the new adjustment of the balance of payments will not be the same as the old, since it has been accompanied by a decline in the rate of *new* foreign investment.

(2) Tariffs affect the situation by altering the relative level of prices and incomes in the areas concerned in international trade. Given an effective rate of tariff duty, imports into the tariff area are checked, whilst exports are not immediately affected. The balance of payments, therefore, is adjusted by means of an inflow of bullion, which raises both prices and the level of money incomes. The result, of course, is that at the higher level of prices and money incomes the importation of bullion ceases and goods take the place of gold. But, if the renewed inflow of goods leads to a further heightening of the tariff wall, the result must necessarily be a further accretion of gold, until the price and income structure becomes sufficiently raised to enable the liquidation of the balance in goods.

This process is, of course, assisted by the circumstance that, as gold flows into the tariff area and flows out of other areas, their price and income structure may (and in normal cases will) be altered, so that a stimulus to their exports and a check to their imports takes place. But, if the gold flows are *not* allowed to influence the price and income structure in either area, the tariff, in the one case, and the rigidity of the cost and income structure in both cases, may become the cause of a quasi-permanent drain of gold; and the original equilibrium position of the balance of payments will not be attained. (There are, of course, other effects of a tariff on individual prices and on the flow of individual commodities which cannot be dealt with here.)

(3) Interest and capital payments are constituents of the balance of payments of the greatest importance in the modern world. If the economic machine is functioning adequately, imports of capital take the concrete shape of an excess of imports over exports, or, what is the same thing, they permit of an increase of imports without a corresponding increase in exports or of the maintenance of the same volume of imports with an actual decline in the volume of exports. Interest payments result in an excess of exports over imports, or, what is the same thing, they involve the maintenance of exports even if imports fall, or an increase of exports if imports remain stable. To produce these results, however, the price and income structure has to be adapted to meet the needs of the situation.

In the case of capital loans, a *direct* effect is produced by the circumstance that the inhabitants of the borrowing country, as a group, have now more purchasing power at their immediate disposal, whilst the inhabitants of the lending country have, for the moment, parted with their power to dispose of as much purchasing power as before. This must produce some shift in relative prices both in the capital importing and capital exporting countries, which reacts upon the movements of goods inwards and outwards. But such an influence as this may not be sufficient to adjust the situation to the new requirements. If, in the capital exporting country, the price and income structure is inappropriate, in view of the increased exports which are now necessary, the borrowers will attempt to convert their claims which are in terms of money into gold, so as to be able to buy elsewhere the goods they need, or part of them. This sets up the reactions already dealt with elsewhere.

Again, since the loans enable payment to be made for imports which would otherwise have to be paid for by exports, the effects of a loan may be, not to lower the price and income structure in the capital exporting country, but to permit a higher level of money incomes and prices to be maintained in the capital importing country than would otherwise be possible. This *higher* level of prices and incomes *checks* exports, whilst it leaves imports at a higher level than would otherwise be possible.

It follows from this that a sudden check to capital loans imposes a great strain upon capital importing areas, since it forces them either to adjust their price and income structure to a level at which they can pay for the imports which they formerly borrowed, or to check their imports.

What has been said of capital movements can be applied *mutatis mutandis* to interest payments. In order that interest payments may be effected, the price and income structure has to be lower in the interest-paying country or be higher in the interest-receiving country than it need otherwise be. It also follows from what has previously been said that a country in the receipt of interest payments will be forced to a change in its price and income structure in a downward direction if these suddenly stop because, if it still wishes to import as much as it did before, it must now export more than it did before. Similarly, a country which ceases to have interest payments to make can then sustain a higher price and cost structure than it did before because, whilst its imports remain the same, it no longer requires the same volume of exports.

The adjustments necessary in order that capital and interest payments can be made *need* not, however, be made: there is nothing in the theory of international equilibrium which implies this. They may not be made because the monetary authorities are unwilling or unable to initiate the process of adjustment or because the necessity of making them may be for a time avoided by special devices and expedients. Interest may be met by dissipation of reserves accumulated in the past or by borrowing for that special purpose. Capital movements which, to be effective, might have involved a downward direction of the price and income structure, are prevented from having this effect by counter-borrowing, so that, from the final economic point of view, the two movements cancel out.

All that has just been said applies with especial force to the transfer of reparations. A transfer of reparations involves an adjustment of the price and income structure in both the paying and the recipient areas. The collection of the proceeds of the taxation necessary for the purpose of raising the reparations due leads to a relative decline in certain prices, through the transfer of the amounts so raised to foreigners. This in itself leads to changes in the structure of production and, since the purchasing power, e.g., of the German people is reduced, to a decline in imports. But, if these shifts are not sufficient, again German currency falls to a discount in the market and gold flows abroad. If this is followed by price and income declines in Germany and by rises elsewhere, an excess of exports equal to the amount to be transferred will ultimately result. But this process may be 'short circuited' by borrowing, in the countries to which reparations are due, a part or the whole of what is owing to them. In that case no adjustment in the desired direction takes place; on the contrary, if more is borrowed abroad than is required for reparations purposes, the German price and income structure moves in the opposite direction, so that, if borrowing ceases, the degree of adjustment necessary becomes even greater than it need originally have been.

To sum up. The international gold standard supplies the world with a mechanism for maintaining fixity of exchange and for keeping in organic touch with one another the price and income structures of the various countries. But the degree to which the second of these functions is in fact adequately performed depends, not on the mere existence of a common currency basis, but on the manner in which the detailed administration of the gold standard in each and all of the countries adhering to it is carried out. This necessarily leads to an investigation of the manner in which the gold standard has actually been functioning in the recent past and to a consideration of the various criticisms to which its actual working has given rise.

CHAPTER II

THE WORKING OF THE GOLD STANDARD IN RECENT YEARS

THE INTERNATIONAL gold standard is a device for securing fixity of exchange rates and maintaining an integrated price and income structure over the whole range of gold standard countries. But it is something more than this: it is truer to say, much more than this. In the nineteenth century the necessity for a metallic basis to the currency system was taken for granted; the only preoccupation of currency theorists was with the choice of the metal to serve as the basis, and the commercial predominance of Great Britain, combined with the happy chance of the great gold discoveries, settled this issue at the expense of dethroning silver from its former position of authority. But, with the adoption of the gold standard, the long-period price level was also tied to gold, and gold thus became the international standard of deferred payments. This was and is a fact of great and of growing significance. All economists would agree that long-period changes in the value of money are responsible for *some* disturbance to the economic system, and some economists would further agree that long-period changes in the value of money are *solely* responsible for the major disturbances to the even flow of economic operations. The effects of changes in the value of money, that is, the effects of changes in the price level, require careful examination.

The social and economic consequences of changes in the purchasing power of money, whether these are on balance good or bad, are *due* to the impossibility of adjusting the rate of change of particular price series to one another with sufficient rapidity and comprehensiveness. The magnitude of the social and economic consequences are in proportion, therefore, not only to the absolute magnitude of the price changes themselves, but to the ease or difficulty with which the economic system can adjust itself to them. Consider first, the relation between price changes and *costs*. When the prices of products fall, without a change in the efficiency of production having first taken place and without a change in wage rates or other charges, the margin of profit to the business man falls also, and he is forced either to suspend production altogether or to restrict it, because his money income falls without any change in his outgoings. A sharp fall of prices leads inevitably therefore to a growth in the volume of unemployment, and this increased unemployment will persist, unless and until the money incomes paid to those who assist in production fall, whether through the provision of labour services or of capital or capital goods, or unless the fall in the price level is compensated by an increase in the efficiency of industry. To put the matter somewhat differently, a fall in prices has the effect of checking production and of redistributing the proceeds of industry in such a way as to increase the share of those whose money receipts have not declined at the expense of those whose incomes do decline. It is true that, if efficiency increases during and as a consequence of depression, the decline in the price level may be compensated.

The degree to which the money incomes of those who assist in production remains fixed depends upon the specific terms of the contract, in the first instance, upon bargaining power and upon custom. In one sense none of them is fixed; for if labour is discharged or a works is closed down and the fixed plant and machinery are sold as scrap iron, there is an end to any income at all.

But, assuming that production is in part still carried on, those are directly affected whose only claim to continue to receive their usual income is based on custom or a short-dated contract, whilst those are least immediately affected whose incomes are protected (as those, e.g., of debenture holders are) by long-term contracts. But in recent years the general resistance to change has become strengthened. The bargaining power of the workers and their ability to resist 'cuts' have increased in consequence of the existence of the dole. The consequence has necessarily been an increase in the volume of unemployment.

Once a depression has been initiated it tends to perpetuate itself; for the decline in productivity, however initiated, tends to affect one industry and branch of employment after another. This occurs partly because the growth of unemployment is a direct cause of the reduction of demand for consumption goods, partly because orders for raw materials fall off and partly because the decline in business profits and the discouraging outlook check the flotation of new loans. In this way the demand for the products of the heavy constructional industries is also affected and, in fact, experience shows that it is proportionally more affected than the demand for consumers' goods. The purchasing power of those incomes which are still received and which are fixed in terms of money or which fall less rapidly than the price level falls steadily rises, but the aggregate national income, in terms of money, declines.

The economic system operates within a territorial framework and the financial activities of the modern State are also profoundly affected by changes in the price level. Budgetary equilibrium is bound to be affected; for on the revenue side income from taxation falls off as trade and production decline, whilst a large part of the expenditure of every modern State is fixed in terms of money and cannot be easily altered. This is true both of the interest upon the National Debt and of money payments incurred under the heading of the Social Services. Conversion operations can gradually effect a reduction of the burden of debt charges, and 'economy campaigns' can gradually modify the cost of the Social Services; but, as recent events have shown, only at the high cost of exacerbating class antagonism. So long as these burdens remain and the depression persists, any of the methods by which the Budget can be balanced has unfavourable consequences of its own. Higher taxation exercises depressing psychological effects and increases the difficulty of Debt conversion; borrowing raises the rate of interest on Government loan-operations and also has unfavourable effects both upon psychology and the chances of Debt conversion; there are obvious limits to economies achieved by reduction of expenditure in other directions. These difficulties become accentuated when the bulk of the indebtedness is due to foreigners, not only on the technical economic ground that relative price changes as between the products of the creditor and debtor nation may increase the difficulty of producing the requisite 'export surplus' but *also* because economies forced on a people in the interests of foreign creditors are bound to be even more unpopular than economy in general is apt to be. Hence financial difficulties are often followed by political instability and in the end, as we have seen in the case of South America particularly, by revolution. The effect of falling prices (again in the absence of technical changes which allow the maintenance of money incomes even in the face of falling prices) is, so far as Public Finance is concerned, to transfer to those beneficiaries of State expenditure whose incomes do not vary as the price level varies a larger proportion of the national income than before.

It is easy to see why, when faced with the intolerable difficulties of public finance in periods of depression, Government should fall back upon the expedient of abandoning the gold standard, since this gives it the immediate opportunity of checking the fall of prices, though it may bring in its train difficulties and dangers even greater than those which it seeks to avoid. But, though a departure from the gold standard may alleviate the immediate difficulties, it does not follow that they have been *caused* by the existence of the gold standard. Nor does it follow, even if the particular difficulties of a falling price level had been directly caused by the existence of the gold standard, that, if the gold standard had not existed since the War, difficulties of another and an even more intolerable kind would not have arisen. It must not for a moment be forgotten that the rebirth of the gold standard after the War was directly due to the consequences of the working of free paper standards during the War and the immediate post-War period.

The question whether the gold standard had in fact been responsible for the existing depression and all its consequences remains, nevertheless, an issue of the greatest possible importance upon which it is most desirable to have clear ideas. If this were a matter to be settled by the mere use of authority, the matter might perhaps be disposed of by citing the contrary view expressed by the Macmillan Committee.[1] But it

[1] Comd. 3897 of 1931, paragraphs 208–9: '. . . The economic difficulties of the post-War decade are primarily due, not to any wanton misbehaviour on the part of the monetary factors themselves but to unusually large and rapid changes on the part of what are rightly described as non-monetary phenomena, these non-monetary factors again themselves producing monetary

is much better to analyse the contention than summarily to dismiss it. The statement is in fact ambiguous. It may mean:

(1) That the gold standard has caused the present depression because the existence of that standard has involved the presence of at least two factors which would not have been present if some other standard had obtained, viz., a gold shortage and a maldistribution of gold, and these two factors are capable of explaining the present depression.

(2) That grave mistakes have been committed in the administration of the gold standard.

(3) That, though administered with as much technical skill and goodwill as was possible under the circumstances, the gold standard is not easily compatible with the conditions of the post-War world in certain respects, owing to the emergence of new circumstances of which insufficient notice has been taken.

The second of these assertions is, of course, perfectly compatible with the third; and the third is, of course, in itself perfectly compatible with the view that the gold standard is so necessary a piece of international mechanism that, instead of abandoning it because of its incompatibility with certain other phenomena of the post-War world, the utmost possible should be done to modify these other circumstances in order to place the international gold standard on a firmer foundation. The remainder of the present chapter is concerned with an examination of the validity of the contention that it is not in the mere existence of the gold standard but in the mode of its working under the peculiar

changes. . . . The recent world-wide fall of prices is best described as a monetary phenomenon which has occurred as the result of the monetary system failing to solve successfully a problem of unprecedented difficulty and complexity set it by a conjunction of highly intractable non-monetary phenomena.'

circumstances of the post-War world that the key to the present situation is to be found.

The view that the depression was due *directly* to an absolute gold shortage cannot be sustained. It is true that the mere fact that the total gold stocks of Central Banks and Treasuries of the world as a whole have steadily increased in recent years is not evidence that there has not been an absolute shortage of gold. For under modern conditions, when gold is no longer in active circulation over the greater part of the civilized world, the only uses to which it can be put are to serve as the basis of credit or of note issue, to be used in the industrial arts or to be hoarded in the East. So long as the absolute output of new gold from the mines is greater than the total quantity of gold used in the industrial arts or the East, or so long as there is any gold still in circulation which can be gradually commandeered by Central Banks or Treasuries—even if the non-monetary consumption is equal to or exceeds the current output of new gold—there must be an increase in the total *visible* gold holdings of the world. The issue can only be settled by an appeal to the known fact that between 1925 and 1929 the world was passing through an epoch of great economic progress. The gold supplies and the volume of purchasing power built upon those supplies must have been sufficient to support that advance, for it in fact took place. No change in the supply of gold has since taken place sufficient to explain the altered circumstances. Even if the *absolute* supply of gold had been greater throughout the period of economic expansion and contraction, there is no reason to suppose that the absolute degree of contraction between one period and another would have been less; for either the Banks might have maintained higher reserve ratios at all relevant times (without, therefore, any influence being exerted upon the level of prices through a change in the volume of purchasing power) or the price level might indeed have been higher before the break, but the rate of price decline subsequently might have been much the same as it has in fact proved to be.[1]

The view that the depression is due to 'gold maldistribution' rests upon a more plausible basis. The mere *fact* of gold redistribution proves nothing, of course, since the redistribution may be an effect, and not a cause, of change. The concentration of gold has been, in fact, much more marked in the last few years, after the depression had already begun, which suggests that the gold redistribution could not have been the initiating feature. The depression has released forces, e.g., renewed uncertainty as to the future position of various currency systems, which have *produced* gold drains. In other cases the gold drains are due to the impossibility of raising fresh loans or selling produce at remunerative prices and so to pressure to adjust the 'balance of payments' by gold shipments at a time when it was impossible, or thought to be so, to reduce the local income structure by deflationary steps; in other cases, again, the depression has forced the abandonment of the gold standard and enabled the gold reserves to be used without any effect on the local price situation. In all these cases the gold flows may have helped to accentuate the depression, but they did not initiate it.

It may be argued that what is true of the years since

[1] What has been said above is quite consistent with the view that ever since the end of the War the secular trend of prices has been downwards and that part of the difficulty of *recovering* from the present depression is due to this circumstance. But as an explanation of the sharp alteration of the situation in 1929 even this more plausible (and, in my opinion, correct) statement of the gold position will not serve.

1929 is not true of the year 1929 itself. In that year the heavy flows of gold to New York and to Paris led to an orgy of bank-rate changes in Europe, and these changes, by causing dear money, *produced* the depression. But this view is only tenable on the assumption that the seeds of the depression had not already been sown in the shape of the American boom. At most, the bank-rate changes of 1929 brought about the collapse somewhat sooner than would otherwise have been the case by preventing a further outflow of funds to the New York money market. The peak of industrial production had already been passed in America, and the decline of production marked the beginning of the end of the era of prosperity. The gold flows of 1929 were doubtless a factor of some importance in the general situation, but they were only one among several: of which the business situation in the United States outranged all others in significance. The American boom which, while it lasted, sustained, and in its turn was sustained by, boom conditions in other countries, itself calls for analysis and explanation. There can be little question that it was *initiated* by the cheap money policy of the Federal Reserve System in the winter of 1927–8, and that its unusual *amplitude* was due to the reluctance on the part of the American banking authorities to intervene except at an advanced stage when successful intervention had become difficult. But, since the cheap money policy was initiated, not only to assist the American business world to overcome the depression of 1927, but also to help the European gold standard countries at a time when gold threatened to go to America, it ill becomes Europeans to throw too many stones at the Federal Reserve System. It is more profitable to turn to a consideration of the general nature of the post-War economic situation and to discuss how and why this situation complicated the working of the gold standard.

In the first place, the economic life of the world has been subjected throughout the whole period to an unprecedented degree of political influence. It is a truism that planning and preparing for the future involves confidence in the future; but that confidence has in the last decade been lacking for the greater part. At the present moment there is complete uncertainty as to the future political relations between France and Germany, the future of German domestic politics and the whole outlook for European peace. No doubt the uncertainty was partly the reflex of unfavourable economic conditions and became aggravated as the economic situation became worse, whilst the partial recovery of 1933–4 has not gone far enough to alleviate matters. But it was a deterrent factor throughout, *preventing* the machinery of long-period investment from functioning adequately and thus forcing on the method of financing by short-term credits which has proved so dangerous a factor in times of tension. But, in consequence of the impoverishment of Europe as a result of war and inflation, the degree to which certain European countries are dependent upon foreign loans has greatly increased. The political factor has forced lending to assume the form most likely to embarrass the working of the banking machine.

Secondly, the world inherited from the era of violent inflation which preceded the restoration of the gold standard a heightened awareness of the possibility of a currency becoming worthless. The result was that the international banking machine, in moments of political or economic tension, had to cope not only with the withdrawals of credit by outside lenders, but also with the demands for foreign currency by those who wished to flee from the local currency. And, at all times, the feeling of nervousness has taken the form of desiring to hold reserves in a 'liquid' form. There has been a reluctance to venture savings and so expose them to the dangers of renewed inflation. This has thrown upon the banks a technical problem of great difficulty; since if, for any reason, holders of liquid resources (i.e. bank deposits) suspected the banks, they subjected them to unusual pressure; whilst the banks, by investing 'long' if they borrowed 'short', were of course courting the very dangers they wished to avoid; if they refused to invest at all, or only on short term, they aggravated the general business situation. The abnormally wide margin between rates of interest on long-term and short-term loans which has been characteristic of Europe in the last decade and a half is no accident: it is a measure, not only of a shortage of capital, but also of the risks which it was feared attached to lending on long-term.

Thirdly, the world economic structure has become rigid to an unprecedented degree. Owing to the much greater pressure which organized business and labour interests can bring to bear on Government, there has been a general advocacy of 'stability' which has in practice meant that particular groups could stabilize their own position without any, or enough, attention having been paid to the result of such stabilizing action on other parts of the economic field or to the long-period results of such action. Raw material producers have been allowed, with the aid of Governmental or quasi-Governmental assistance, to 'stabilize' the prices of particular raw materials, without regard to the fact that consumption might thereby be discouraged and production encouraged. In industry and distribution there has been a growth of large-scale organizations which have not always been willing to adjust prices to the trend of the market, thus adding in the end to the losses which had to be suffered on stocks when liquidation finally became necessary. The depression has accentuated these factors in the economic organization of the world. In the sphere of labour there has been in certain countries a development of unemployment insurance schemes or similar relief measures which have prevented wage rates from falling, whilst in others public opinion, reinforced by Government propaganda, has had very much the same effect. In a word, there have been tendencies at work in many countries preventing a rapid adjustment of the level of money incomes to changes in the general economic situation. Where the level of money incomes at the moment when the gold standard was originally restored was a low one, as, e.g., particularly in France and Italy, a certain 'margin of tolerance' was present, for adjustment could come, not by forcing the level of money incomes down, but by slackening the rate at which the movement upwards took place. From the standpoint of the working of the international gold standard, such a rigidity of social structure and of the scale of money income implied that the adjustment, which might under more elastic conditions have been made by movements in the domestic price and income structure, was at best *delayed*, with the inevitable effect that gold movements, or, what is in the modern world very much the same thing, changes in the holding of foreign exchange assets at the command of the Central Bank, took place on a larger scale than would otherwise have been necessary. At worst, the adjustments were not made at all. For a time it was attempted to prop up the situation by loans, short or long. This enabled a larger volume of consumption of foreign goods to continue for a longer time than would have been possible otherwise; i.e. the balance of payments remained uncorrected, and, since borrowing could not go on indefinitely, the degree of adjustment finally called for was actually greater than it would otherwise have been.

Lastly, so far as the general nature of the post-War economic situation is concerned, it may be pointed out that the tendency of tariffs to increase has also increased the difficulties of adjustment. For, as already pointed out above (p. 17), tariffs encourage gold imports at the expense of an importation of goods; or, to put it in another way, require a higher price and income structure (differences of efficiency being neglected) in order that the same volume of imports may be attracted. A constantly rising tariff wall *prolongs* the drain of gold or increases the pressure which must be exerted on the price and income structure of debtor and exporting nations in order to secure adjustment. But reasons have just been given why such adjustment is more difficult to secure to-day than it was in the pre-War world. In this respect the depression, by encouraging the growth of the quota system at the expense of mere increases in the tariff rate, has made the situation still worse.

We turn now to the question of how far the working of the gold standard, in so far as this turns on the views and policies of Central Banks themselves, was unfavourably affected by the attitude taken up by these banks or by mistakes committed by them from time to time. Here, just as in the case of the attribution of all the difficulties of the situation to 'gold shortage' and 'gold maldistribution', public opinion is inclined to state the situation in far too simple terms: the Central Banks are accused of failure to 'co-operate' and of insensitiveness to the trend of opinion. Neither of these statements, in its *baldest* form, is in the least true. There has in fact been a great deal of co-operation: the European countries returning to the gold standard were assisted to do so by means of stabilization credits; financial reconstruction in Austria, Hungary, and elsewhere was greatly helped by special action by the Bank of England; in the winter of 1927 the Federal Reserve System paid regard to the special needs of Europe; ever since the formation of the Bank for International Settlements the leading Central Banks have been in close touch through the monthly meetings of the Board; in the earlier stages of the depression the Bank for International Settlements advanced huge sums to Germany; the Bank of England came to the assistance of Austria, and both France and the U.S.A. to the assistance of Great Britain. Later still, before the American collapse, France and the United States reached an agreement for the purpose of protecting the American dollar. It is true that co-operation has been made more difficult by the intrusion at times of political elements; that sometimes agreement was achieved only after the situation it was intended to remedy had become much worse in consequence of delay: and that, in general, the criticism may be passed that there has not been among Banks sufficient prevision of what failure to stabilize the economic position would involve. In other cases, no doubt, failure to reach agreement was due to real differences of opinion as to the right course of action to pursue or to real short-run differences of interest between money markets. But such difficulties as these are inevitable and do not justify a general charge of absence of co-operation. As regards the influence of public opinion, it is at least arguable that the Central Banks have been over-inclined to pay attention to it; public opinion and the exigencies of a Presidential election prevented the Federal Revenue System from putting on the screw early enough to prevent the disastrous boom in the United States; the Bank of England was forced into the policy offsetting gold losses and encouraging foreign balances at least in part by the clamour of those who saw disaster in every rise of the Bank rate; the Bank of France has, it is stated, been forced to act at times as the instrument of French foreign policy (what justification there is for this charge, commonly levelled in the British and American financial Press, is another matter); the Reichsbank, even before the collapse, had to fight a sharp battle to get enforced some control over German foreign borrowings. These illustrations will at least serve to refute the allegation of indifference to public opinion, though conformity to public opinion is hardly the best test of the correctness of Central Bank action. In truth the problem is much more complicated.

There has, to begin with, been a general tendency to fix minimum reserve ratios at too high a figure; this has meant that Central Banks have had to keep effective reserves considerably higher than those which they needed to have kept otherwise. As a consequence public opinion has become unnecessarily excited when gold flows or foreign exchange drains began, as in the case of the Reichsbank and, more recently, in the case of the Federal Reserve Banks. But it is not always realized that small gold stocks or smaller foreign exchange reserves can be kept only if the process of international adjustments is allowed to work itself out quickly and if there is no danger of vast amounts of liquid capital being suddenly withdrawn. But, as already pointed out, the speedy adjustment of international balances of payment has been much impeded in post-War years by the growing rigidity of the social and economic structure: and the sensitiveness of the International Short Loan Market to political influences has been one of the greatest difficulties of the last few years. In any case, it must be remembered that the increased use made of the gold exchange standard, by which foreign gold assets and not actual gold is held in reserve, itself represents a considerable economy of gold. It is one of the misfortunes resulting from Great Britain's departure from the gold standard that great losses must have been inflicted on those Central Banks keeping balances here in the London Market, so that this particular instrument of gold economy is likely to suffer a considerable setback in popularity.

It is also probably the case that the Central Banks have not sufficiently considered the dangers involved in the devices of which much has been heard during the recent decade: i.e. 'offsetting' and 'sterilizing'. By the first device gold or foreign exchange losses are prevented from affecting the basis of credit by an extension of the earning assets of the Central Bank (its loans and discounts); by the second device accretions of gold are prevented from raising the price level by a sale by the Central Bank of some of its earning assets. But, if one set of countries sterilizes gold imports and another group offsets gold exports, the international price and income structure is *prevented* from adjusting itself rapidly, for prices and incomes will not fall in the one case, and will not rise in the other. In other words, given these devices, a greater volume of gold will have to flow, or a greater loss of foreign exchange reserves will have to be sustained, before a given degree of approximation in the price and income structures of the two areas is attained. Central Bank policy reinforces, by the use of these devices, the influence of those other elements in the situation which work against speedy international adjustment. The development of these devices was a natural result of the growing desire, which has affected bankers as well as politicians and business men, to interpose some obstacle to the speedy communication of impulses from without to a given national economy. But unquestionably also all such devices impede the smooth working of the international gold standard.

To sum up: the post-War world is in some important respects markedly different from the pre-War world, notably in the degree to which political influences exert a deterrent effect on the developments of economic life and in the extent to which the greater rigidity and inelasticity of the economic structure impose obstacles to the adjustment of relative incomes and prices. The working of the gold standard, as an instrument of enforcing international equilibrium, has suffered from these as from other elements in the present world situation—notably the insufficient degree to which the normal relations between the long-term and the short-term money markets have been restored. Neither gold shortage, gold maldistribution, nor lack of Central Bank co-operation is sufficient to explain the unsatisfactory character of the general economic situation. The fall of prices must primarily be regarded as the reaction from the world boom of 1925–9, a boom which was itself prolonged by the failure to take earlier steps to correct it. The appearance of certain new banking devices has probably on balance assisted to prevent speedy adjustment of the international situation. Economy in the case of gold, though assisted by the development of the gold exchange mechanism, has been impeded, not only by the nature of the reserve legislation adopted since the War, which requires the Banks in fact to hold reserves substantially above the legal minima, but also by the existence of an abnormally large International Short-Loan Fund. This Fund is capable by its sudden movement of very rapidly depleting a reserve and of thus adding a new element of uncertainty to an already complicated situation.

CHAPTER III

THE CASE OF GREAT BRITAIN: THE CAUSES OF THE BREAKDOWN

THE CAUSES which drove Great Britain off the gold standard are complex, since they involve elements both near and remote in time. Political controversy, by seizing on the elements in the situation most proximate in time, and by imparting to the whole discussion a note of personal and class vilification, succeeded in conveying to vast masses of people who for the first time had to concern themselves with problems of currency an utterly distorted picture, both of the working of the international financial machine and of the forces which brought about the final conjuncture of events.

The beginnings of the crisis may be traced back to 1925, when the gold standard was restored. At that time controversy turned on the question of whether or not the rate of exchange ruling before the War between the gold pound and the gold dollar should be the rate to be adopted in the future: whether, in other words, the pre-War ratio between the pound and gold should be restored. The point insisted upon by the opponents of the return to the gold standard at the old parity was simply that the dollar rate of exchange had been rising very rapidly, and that there was considerable reason to suppose that this rise was *not* due to anything more fundamental than an anticipation on the part of American speculators that the pound would be linked up again with gold at the old ratios. But, whilst the dollar value of sterling was rising rapidly, the internal level of money incomes was not falling: in other words, if the rise in the dollar value of the pound sterling was to be made *permanent*, this would result in an over-valuation of the pound in terms of its domestic purchasing power, which, unless corrected by a subsequent increase of efficiency or a fall in money incomes, would be bound to have disadvantageous effects upon the British balance of payments. For an increase in the dollar (and gold) value of sterling of, say, 10 per cent, would be equivalent to an increase in the cost (to the foreigner) of all British exports of 10 per cent; whilst a similar rise in the purchasing power of sterling in terms of gold or dollar would be equivalent to a fall in the cost of all foreign imports to inhabitants of this country. Unless the cost of British goods, in terms of pounds, *fell* by 10 per cent, or the prices of foreign goods, in terms of foreign currency, *rose* by 10 per cent, then an improvement of 10 per cent in the purchasing power of the British pound in terms of gold or foreign currencies themselves convertible into gold would encourage imports at the expense of exports, i.e. it would force an alteration in the constituents of the British balance of payments which would involve the country in grave difficulties. For, in order to secure equilibrium, it would be necessary either (1) to increase efficiency by an amount sufficient to overcome the initial disadvantage of sterling costs being too high by, say, 10 per cent; or (2) to reduce the average level of costs by, say, 10 per cent; or (3) to adjust the volume of British capital exports in such a way as to take account of the fact that a larger proportion of the imports into the country would have to be paid for out of the proceeds of shipping earnings and interest on past investments, which would leave a smaller margin available for re-investment; or (4) lastly, if none of these adjustments were possible, it would be necessary to face the prospect of an increase in the volume of unemployment in the export industries and the constant danger of the Central Bank battling with a loss of gold, which in its turn would involve 'dear money'. Dear money *might*, in its turn, check capital exports and, through the pressure on employers, *force* on a battle for wage reductions between them and their employees. But the issue in such a conflict was uncertain. If the attempt to reduce the average level of remuneration were unsuccessful, a continued stagnation in British exports was inevitable.

The 10 per cent 'over-valuation' of the pound, which has been taken as a purely illustrative figure in the preceding paragraph, has, as a matter of historical record, played a predominant role in the shaping of opinion. It is as well, then, to remind the reader of the original source of the calculation. It was not an official estimate at all, but appeared in the course of controversial articles published by Mr. J. M. Keynes, the basis of the calculation being a comparison of the British and Massachusetts cost of living indices. Using these two sets of figures, the inference drawn was perfectly valid.[1] But a comparison of the British cost of living index with the American Bureau of Labour index for the cost of living in the United States as a whole would have yielded precisely the opposite result, i.e. it would have shown that the British pound, before the return to the gold standard at the rate of $4·866 U.S. to the pound, was actually during 1924 worth about 10 per cent less in terms of dollars than it ought to have been worth. The immediate results of the return to the gold standard were consistent with *either* view—with the view that this step led to an over-valued exchange or with the view that the parity actually chosen ended

[1] All the relevant statistical material will be found at p. 52 et seq. of my *First Year of the Gold Standard*. (London 1926.)

a period of under-valuation. For a rise in the international value of the pound, without any adjustment of the internal level of costs, was bound in any case to throw an increased strain upon the exporting industries.

The disabilities to which the export industries were exposed were not slow in making themselves felt, but it would be a complete misconception to suppose that all the difficulties which have been encountered during the course of the following six years are to be attributed *directly* to the exchange position as it was at the beginning of the period. A most complicated economic and political situation cannot be so simply explained.

The first effect of the rise in the value of sterling naturally was to cause staple exports to fall off in value and volume, thereby creating unemployment in those industries, and, as time went on, to cause the level of wages in these trades to fall substantially below the general level. But this very reduction should have assisted to bring about a recovery, even though ancillary costs did not fall. But the older export industries were additionally handicapped by the emergence of new competitive conditions and by a shift in the nature of world demand. The stabilization of the Belgian, French, and Polish currencies at a level which substantially *under-valued* the currency (i.e. left their prices in terms of gold unduly low); the emergence of aggravated Japanese competition in the Far East, coupled with the Indian boycott and the world-stagnation in demand for certain textile products and for coal, adversely affected the iron and steel, coal, cotton, and woollen industries and, to a lesser extent, the engineering industries; and these *were* the staple trades of the country, dependent largely upon exports for a continuance of prosperous conditions. Had the pound been stabilized in 1925 at a lower figure it would have removed one initial handicap (assuming that it would not, by encouraging the Continental countries who stabilized subsequently to do so at a *still* lower rate, have given them a still greater exchange advantage), but the others would have remained.

So large a proportion of British pre-War foreign trade was done by these staple industries that their continued stagnation very much impressed both British public opinion and Continental critics, with the result that insufficient attention was paid to the position of the other export industries. As a matter of fact, out of the twenty groups of commodities into which British exports of articles wholly or mainly manufactured are divided twelve show an increase over 1913, whilst eight show a decline, comparing 1929 with the last pre-War years. But the improvement in the position of these twelve groups was not sufficient to outweigh *quantitatively* the effect of the decline in the quantity of exports in the other eight groups. Great Britain's exporting capacity was prejudiced, partly by the fact that her predominant pre-War export industries were being subjected to special difficulties and partly by the rise in the external value of sterling, which not only accentuated the pressure on these particular industries but hampered the possibilities of expansion of the other exporting industries. Whilst wage rates fell in certain exporting industries, e.g. in coal-mining and engineering, this fall was not accompanied necessarily by such a general fall in all their costs, direct and indirect, as to lead to a reduction of export prices by an amount equal to a given fall in the wage rate, since wages constitute only part of the total cost, and not always even the largest proportionate part of the total costs, of a given product.

But this problem of the export industries—which was only in part a problem of the rate of exchange—really raised another problem of a far more fundamental character. Why did not the labour which could no longer find employment in the export industries move into other industries? The answer is by no means simple. Firstly, labour transfer upon a considerable scale *did* take place; secondly, some labour which was *willing* to move could not move either because of unsuitability for the kind of job offered, or because of ignorance of where work could be got, or because of lack of adequate accommodation in the areas (mostly in the South of England) where the newer industries were settling down. The question is whether these causes of non-transference exhaust the reasons why not more labour was actually transferred. Was there not also some *unwillingness* to transfer, in spite of an ability to do so? A reluctance to move, so long as any hope remains of finding a job in an accustomed trade, is a perfectly natural feeling. The existence of the Unemployment Insurance Acts works towards a strengthening of this feeling. But there is another aspect of the problem. A single individual can plead, and with justice plead, that he can find no work available at the rate of wages to which he is accustomed; such work may not in fact exist. It does not follow that there is no work of any kind available of the sort which he is capable of doing. But if there is hope that he may one day find work at the old rate of wages in his old occupation, if there is a strong class-feeling that wage reductions or acceptance of lower wage rates are *intrinsically* undesirable, and if, at the same time, at least a bare minimum of existence is guaranteed by the existence of the 'dole', it would be foolish to expect unemployment to disappear. The workman resents the suggestion that he prefers the 'dole' to work, and he is right in doing so. But, unfortunately, what he means and what his critic very often means are two different things. The critic means that working-class sentiment has enforced the rule that it is better to accept the 'dole' than a job at lower than the normal rate, and that this is a cause of unemployment. The workman means that, if he could get a job at the rate to which he is accustomed, he would accept it rather than the 'dole'. But, since the number of jobs which can pay a certain rate of wage is at any moment limited, a willingness to work at that rate is not evidence that unemployment is not in part caused by the existence of too high rates of wages, in the sense that, if workers were willing to accept lower rates, more jobs would be in fact available. What these jobs are cannot be foretold in advance, for they are in fact *created* by the offer to accept a lower rate of pay. Thus there is some reason to think that the absence of greater flexibility of wage rates explains, in part, the continuance of unemployment, although that unemployment was concentrated in the main in a few leading industries.

The question as to what rate of wages can be paid by industry in order to absorb the whole of the existing volume of unemployment (in technical terms, the marginal rate of wages) is complicated by changes in the productivity of industry as a whole. The evidence available points to a considerable increase in *per capita* productivity during the period under discussion—about 10 per cent, if not more. Now an increase in productivity per head allows more wages to be paid to those still employed in the industries where the increase in efficiency is being experienced. But it does not necessarily follow that the *whole* of the increase in productivity is available for increased wage payments, since additional capital will have had to be employed which itself requires remuneration. Nor does it follow that the demand for the products of these industries is so elastic that so many more people can be employed as to absorb those whose livelihood is threatened by improvements, for these have been introduced *because*, at the existing level of wage rates, capital was a more economical agent of production to use than labour. An increased output per head of those still employed is therefore no proof that the same rate of wages can be paid to those out of employment as to those in employment. It is not even a proof that the rate of wages which would have absorbed all the unemployed before the relative change in efficiency took place will *now* be low enough to absorb them all; for the number to be absorbed has increased. It is the case that, whilst increases of efficiency due to substitution may be going on, labour may also be becoming more efficient *on other grounds*, e.g. the fear of unemployment may, at a given level of wages, cause the worker to produce more than he did before. *Such* a change, by diminishing the relative attractiveness of employing more labour-saving machinery and increasing the attractiveness of employing more labour, *may* raise the marginal rate of wages at which unemployment would cease or prevent it from falling below what it previously was. Such changes in efficiency have in fact also occurred, e.g. in coal-mining.

The economic problem in Great Britain in the years 1925–31 was thus an excessively complicated one, for it comprehended two elements of quite dissimilar kinds. One was concerned with the relative level of costs in Great Britain and abroad, contrasted with one another at any moment through the existing rate of exchange. A reduction of costs in this country, relatively to costs elsewhere, however brought about, whether through a fall of exchange or a rise of costs in other countries or by means of improved processes in the export industries here, would have improved our competitive position.

The other problem was concerned with the difficulty of re-absorbing labour, released in one direction, into new channels. This was a problem in equilibrium: in the relative productivity, at given wage rates and at a given rate of interest, of labour and capital. A mere increase in the volume of purchasing power would *not* have solved this problem; for the volume of purchasing power does not determine in any way the equilibrium rate of wages necessary for the elimination of unemployment.

It was not to be expected that questions of this order of complexity, upon which acute differences of opinion were and are entertained even in professional economic circles, should have been fully and satisfactorily analysed by public opinion at home and abroad. What public opinion seized upon was the continued stagnation in the older export industries, the rigidity of wage rates at a time of falling prices, the continuance of unemployment, and the burden of the 'dole'. Public opinion was not even fully aware of the extent to which improvements tending to a reduction of costs were taking place; and the growth of the total occupied population in *actual employment* influenced opinion far less than the failure of unemployment to fall, although, so long as the total number of employed persons continued to increase, stability in unemployment implied a reduction in the urgency of the unemployment problem. The Continent was inclined to think that Great Britain was 'played out'; the working classes corrupted by the 'dole'; the employing class too anxious to be considered gentlemen to make the vigorous effort necessary to pull industry out of its rut; the whole nation too inclined to blame others for its own misfortunes.[1] What the

[1] See, e.g., for the views of a friendly critic, André Siegfried's *England's Crisis*, 1931, pp. 47, 67, 147, and elsewhere. Long before the crisis, in the summer of 1931, the view that 'Great

Continent might think did not matter so long as this country was not in a position where pessimistic views could *in themselves* work mischief; but this ceased to be the case after the War, for reasons it is now necessary to expound.

The instability of European currencies had, as one of its consequences, the phenomenon known as the 'flight from the currency'. This took the form, partly of the holding of actual foreign bank notes by the ordinary citizen, but, over and above that, it led to the accumulation, in centres like Amsterdam, Zurich, and London, of bank balances to the credit of foreign firms, banks and individuals. When the currencies of France, Belgium, and Italy were stabilized, even though the individual owners of these balances desired to withdraw them, they could only do so, in the main, by selling their balances either to banks, or if they were themselves bankers, to the Central Bank. Speculation in, e.g., francs, moreover, added to the volume of such balances; for an American or English speculator paid for his francs in dollars or sterling, thus placing foreign balances at the disposal of banks in France and Belgium. Since the currencies of Europe were generally stabilized at a figure which encouraged an initial trade and stock exchange boom, further sums were accumulated. One of the great centres which held, and holds, such balances is London.

Throughout the fifty years before the War London had been the great, indeed the only, true international financial centre. A large part of the foreign trade of the world had been financed by means of the promises to pay of London banking firms, who 'accepted' bills of exchange representing shipments of goods between all

Britain would follow where Australia had led' was widespread among Continental observers of the British Empire.

parts of the world for a commission, and who expected to receive from the foreign customers, as well as from the British firms, on whose behalf they accepted, sterling remittances to cover the payment of the bills when due. Thus a constant stream of money from abroad was always being poured into London in payment of bills, the proceeds being placed at the disposal of those who had shipped the goods and wanted payment in sterling. In addition, London lent not only its name, but its cash, which was, of course, partly furnished by the foreign remittances received for the payment of bills due in London. At the outbreak of War, so immensely strong was the creditor position of London that, in order to provide sterling to meet immediate obligations due in London, American firms actually bid $7 per £stg. to obtain the pounds they required.

This accretion of foreign balances after the War altered the position by making London more of a debtor centre than she had been before. Immense amounts were now due, not only by foreigners to London, but by London banks and banking firms to foreigners, the amounts so due being increased by the policy pursued at times of deliberately attracting further sums in order to equilibrate the short-run position of sterling. The balances, as soon as we returned to the old standard, were payable in gold, in some cases at once, in others after notice given. It therefore became an object of policy to prevent these balances from being withdrawn quickly, for with a gold standard the fall of the rate of exchange to the point at which it pays to withdraw in gold is very soon reached. The simplest way of making certain of the retention of these balances was to keep the Bank rate and Money Market rates in London at a figure which would encourage the owners of these balances to keep them here; or, at any rate, to ensure that, if one centre, say Paris, called balances in London, another centre, say New York, would be encouraged to bring fresh money here. In this way the position in London became a very complicated one. The encouragement of balances to flow here or remain here meant that, if for any reason the rate of exchange weakened —because for the moment, e.g., long-term loans to foreigners led to their selling pounds abroad and so led to a weakening of sterling, or because the rate at which imports were flowing in put pressure on the money market for remittance—a 'turn of the screw', i.e. a rise in rates paid for foreign balances, would lead to a demand for pounds abroad to increase the amount held in London, and this demand raised the exchange again to a level which reduced the danger of a gold outflow. The capacity of London to lend, both on short-term account and on long, was increased by this system. For, provided the foreign balances were not all withdrawn together, or provided they were not withdrawn at a rate faster than funds could be returned from the centres to which they had been re-lent, the liabilities of London were liquidated at the same time as the liabilities to London were being repaid. But, if a large part of the foreign balances due by London were withdrawn at a rate faster than London assets could be gathered in, and if, in addition, the whole future position of the London money market were regarded by foreign bankers as in danger, the pressure on the gold stocks of the country might become intense.

The British situation was therefore vulnerable from two points of view. The rigidity of the structure and the difficulties of readjustment, internally and externally, were forcing reliance upon the retention of the foreign balances as the method of equilibrating the position of the 'Balance of Payments'; but the very existence of these balances was a potential source of danger, from the technical banking standpoint. They were liable to move if the world situation or the British situation led to a loss of confidence in the London money market, or if, for any reason, a better price were offered for the use of balances in any foreign centre. The first was an abnormal, the second a normal, banking risk. But once the balances started moving, the loss of gold which the movements might entail was itself a cause for further alarm and a cause for further movement in the balances and for a further loss of gold.

What would have been the conditions under which the monetary authorities could have relied to a smaller extent upon the inflow of foreign balances? It must be pointed out, to begin with, that all the available evidence points, not to an increase of reliance upon foreign balances as the crisis approached, but to a diminution. In so far as the crisis of September 1931 was due to the fears of foreigners leading to a withdrawal of balances, it was not because those balances were increasing in size. On the contrary, as compared with the position a few years previously, the statistical position had improved. During the years 1928–30 the net liability of London (i.e. Deposits *plus* Sterling Bills held in London on foreign account *plus* Advances to discount market *less* Sterling Bills accepted on foreign account, which of course have to be covered when due) gradually fell from £302 millions to £274 millions, and at the end of the first quarter of 1931 had fallen still more to £254 millions.[1] Allowing for the fact that the figures

[1] Macmillan Report, p. 112, and Appendix I, Table II, p. 301. These figures exclude (1) sterling bills held by foreign banks in their own custody, (2) British balances abroad. The first would increase, the second diminish, our net liability to foreigners. Later events seem to point to the fact that the net liability to foreigners was greater than the evidence presented to the Committee would indicate.

are incomplete, so that the absolute magnitude of the amounts involved may be greater than appears and the trend downwards may be exaggerated, nevertheless, so far as is known there had been no *progressive increase* in our dependence on foreign balances as a method of achieving equilibrium. The trade depression was responsible, according to the figures of the Macmillan Committee, for a fall between 1928 and March 1931 of nearly £50 millions in British acceptances on foreign account and nearly £100 millions in the deposits and sterling bills held in London on foreign account, i.e. our foreign liabilities fell faster than our foreign assets. But to have depended less on foreign balances would have involved (1) exporting more, or (2) importing less in the shape of goods, or (3) increasing our earnings from interest on investments abroad, or our earnings upon shipping and financial services, or (4) investing less abroad, in so far as a smaller investment abroad would not have involved, as it might probably have done, a smaller export of goods, or (5) to the extent consistent with the safety of the banking structure, a reduction in the size of our gold reserve. Any of these five alternatives would have enabled the Balance of Payments to balance consistently with a reduction in the volume of foreign balances and with a maintenance of the other items making up the Balance of Payments at their actually recorded figure. But it is extremely improbable that the cause, which would have led to any of these items being different from what it actually was, would have left the others unchanged. Had the foreign balances not been available, the Balance of Payments would still have balanced, but we do not know what the quantitative aspects of the items would have been. All that is *probable* is that if the British economic system had not been protected against pressure from without by the existence of the foreign balances, the level of money costs and incomes would have been lower and that this would have (1) discouraged imports and (2) encouraged exports both of goods and services. But it *might* also have been the case that the rigidity of our system was too great. In that case, without the inflow of balances, exchange might never have risen in 1925 and we might never have returned to the gold standard. However that may be, the possibility of attracting foreign balances to this market made the necessity of more fundamental adjustments less urgent for the moment. But could the situation have been indefinitely maintained, even if the adverse factors directly leading to the catastrophe had never manifested themselves?

The answer depends upon the view taken of the repercussion of the world depression upon the position of Great Britain. Between 1925 and 1929 Great Britain had benefited, together with the rest of the world, from the expansion of trade and production. Exports (in terms of money), though never during the subsequent period attaining the levels reached in 1925, recovered up to 1929, after the slump in 1926 due to the General Strike; whilst the interest received upon overseas investments, the earnings of shipping, and the receipts from the performance of financial and other services were all higher by 1929.[1] The result of these tendencies was that the excess of the credit over the debit items (primarily the cost of imports) in the Balance of Payments increased substantially from £54 millions in 1925 to £103 millions in 1929. New overseas issues in the London capital market amounted to £88 millions in 1925 and to £94 millions in 1929. A substantial withdrawal of balances

[1] Statistics of the Balance of Payments will be found in the Statistical Appendix.

could thus be financed without any pressure on the other items in the Balance of Payments.

By 1930 the situation was already changing. Exports (in terms of money) were falling much faster than imports, and the trade depression was beginning to affect the yield of our foreign investments, as well as the income from shipping and financial and other services. The real excess of the credit over the debit items in the Balance of Payments fell to £28 millions, whilst overseas issues had risen to £109 millions. The position was clearly becoming less comfortable. One of the elements alleviating the situation was the extraordinary fall in the unit prices of raw materials, which meant that the country was provisioning itself with food and raw materials on very favourable terms.

World prices continued to fall during 1931. The average quarterly excess of imports of goods and bullion had been £91 millions in 1929, £98 millions in 1930, and (for the first three quarters) £87 millions in 1931. Income from foreign investments and from shipping certainly continued to fall, and various other balancing items on the favourable side of the account—receipts from Reparations Payments, and profits on international trading in securities, etc. (not included in the official estimates)—were also absent during the whole or part of the year. Against this must be set the fact that the volume of new overseas issues, which had amounted to £77 millions in the first three quarters of 1930, had fallen to £45 millions in the first three quarters of 1931. The reduction in the trade balance *plus* the reduction in the volume of the new overseas issue together amount, for the first three quarters of 1931, to £58 millions. In 1930 the estimated income from shipping, financial services, and foreign investments together came to £395 millions; net Government receipts to £19 millions.

A 10 per cent reduction in the 'invisible income' would amount to only £30 millions for the first three quarters, against a reduction in the 'adverse' items of £58 millions. Even if allowance is made for the falling off in Government receipts and a possible increase in imports during the autumn, provided the falling off in invisible income was of the order of 10 per cent as compared with last year, the position would not have been at all desperate, though none too comfortable. A rate of decline of the order of 20 per cent or more would, of course, have meant a more intense pressure. But these speculations, though they suggest that without the financial crisis the situation would not have been as bad as some public utterances would lead one to suppose, are, of course, quite inapplicable to the position which actually developed.

What were the *direct* causes leading to the suspension of the gold standard? They must be divided into two groups.

The first group relates to the development of the domestic situation in Great Britain, culminating in the impression created abroad by the news of the 'Naval Mutiny'. It cannot be too strongly emphasized that even before the spring of 1931 the Continent was inclined to regard the British situation with suspicion. But then occurred the repeated warnings of the Chancellor of the Exchequer of the dangers of the financial situation, coupled with a weak Budget—interpreted as a sign that, bad as the position was, the nation was not prepared to face it; the pessimistic memorandum submitted by Sir Richard Hopkins to the Royal Commission on Unemployment Insurance; the refusal of the Government of the day to deal with the question of unemployment benefit on the lines suggested by the Interim Report of the Commission that it had itself appointed. Then came the heavy gold losses of the Bank in July, following upon the German banking crisis and the raising of the first credits (itself regarded as a sign of weakness); the publication of the May 'Economy' Report and the agitation over its adoption; the announcement that the first credits were exhausted and that fresh and still larger amounts had had to be borrowed; the placing by the new Government of the fight for the pound in the forefront of discussion; finally, and as the culminating point, the exaggerated fears inspired by the news of naval discontent, which naturally led the Continent to suppose that the executive could no longer rely upon its own forces.[1]

No doubt these events would not have startled the Continent so much if contemporaneous events on the Continent had not been of the gravest character. The political outlook in Germany had long been uncertain: the position of the public finances grave. The situation in these respects was not made better by the delays and the bargaining which occurred before the acceptance by France of the moratorium offer made by President Hoover: a delay which destroyed the psychological effects of the offer and prevented the first signs of renewed confidence from being the opening stage in a real recovery of world affairs.

How far the misfortunes of the Austrian *Creditanstalt* and of the German *Nationalbank* were due to mistakes of their own making, how far due to the influence of the deepening depression on the course of industry generally, cannot be investigated here; but the immediate consequences were that the entire banking structure of the

[1] It is said that the publication by the Macmillan Committee of the volume of foreign balances in London alarmed Continental bankers, instead of reassuring them. Upon this point the writer prefers to offer no comment, but he can testify from personal experience to the impression made in Canada and the United States by the news of the 'Mutiny' in the Royal Navy.

two countries was involved, and a complete breakdown was very narrowly averted. Nor was the situation elsewhere too reassuring: the United States was suffering from an epidemic of bank failures and of currency hoarding; sporadic difficulties were being experienced in France. Moreover, the threat to the German banking system was also a threat to the entire international banking system, because Germany was a short-term debtor on a great scale to the United States, to Great Britain, Switzerland, and Holland. The knowledge that large amounts of assets were at least temporarily immobilized must have been a further element weakening the position of London in the eyes of the Continent.[1] There is one last point to be kept in mind. In addition to the deposits maintained in London for commercial purposes, London was also an important holder of deposits for *reserve purposes*, so that any failure of London to meet demands in gold meant that the security behind, e.g. the Dutch currency, was in effect reduced in value. The anxiety of certain Central Banks to draw out gold at a time when gold withdrawals appeared highly embarrassing to the Bank of England must not be put down to blind panic or selfishness on the part of these Banks.

What finally dragged Great Britain off gold was thus an international banking panic, induced partly by the

[1] According to the information given in the Wiggin Report (*The Economist* Reprint, p. 6), the *total* short-term liabilities of twenty-eight German banks (covering 85 per cent of all short-term indebtedness by German banks) was on March 31st 1931, 5,639 million RM., and in the middle of July, 4,393 million RM. Of this amount, the British portion was 1,153 million RM. and 1,051 million RM., or 20·4 and 23·9 per cent respectively (£56·6 and £52·5 millions). Against this must be set the German balances in London of 96 million RM. in July (£4·8 millions). Of the total British loans, 634 million RM. at the earlier date and 900 million RM. at the latter represented acceptance credits.

Continental situation, partly by the domestic situation in this country, and partly by the fear that the Continental situation was reacting disastrously on the safety of the London banks.

These events suggest two questions, so far as Great Britain is concerned. Firstly, could the Bank of England by more vigorous effort have prevented the collapse of the gold standard? Secondly, what is the responsibility of the bankers who 'borrowed at 3 per cent from France and lent at 8 per cent to Germany'? The elucidation of these issues ought to be the topic of a special inquiry, for much that is relevant to an adequate answer has not yet been revealed. But the following queries appear justified already:

Firstly, assuming that, after the gold losses in July, a foreign credit was necessary, should it not have been larger and should it not have been accompanied by (*a*) a wider extension of the *right* to issue uncovered notes and (*b*) a sharper rise in Bank rate?

Secondly, assuming that it was unwise to alarm public opinion during August, but in view of the fact that the first credit was exhausted in that month, would it not have been better to sacrifice a larger part of the remaining gold stocks and push the Bank rate up to the traditional figure of 10 per cent than to borrow a further enormous amount, if it was not absolutely certain that this credit would save the pound?

Thirdly, was it wise to allow public opinion to concentrate so largely upon the question of the future of sterling? Did this not encourage further foreign withdrawals and even cause some domestic demand for foreign exchange?

As regards the second main issue:

Firstly, would it have improved the European situation if Germany had been deprived of the aid of foreign capital, and, further, would not those who now condemn the banks for having lent to Germany been the first to condemn them for not having lent?

Secondly, would it not have simply accelerated the German crisis if more had been withdrawn from Germany between March and July, for, in fact, during this period considerable amounts were withdrawn?

Thirdly, granting that, in the circumstances of Europe and the world during the last few years, short loans to Germany were better than a refusal to lend at all, was sufficient care exercised in all cases with regard to individual loan transactions?

CHAPTER IV

THE CASE OF GREAT BRITAIN: THE CONSEQUENCES OF THE BREAKDOWN

PART I: THEORETICAL ANALYSIS

BY THE Gold Standard Amendment Act, 1931, the Bank of England is no longer obliged to cash British money into gold bars, the direct result being that the gold (or franc) value of the pound sterling is free to vary downwards. Its value in terms of francs or gold may sink to zero, but its value in terms of gold currencies can never *rise* above the point at which the pound is worth rather more than $\frac{480}{1868}$ of an ounce of standard gold, for, if it does, gold will be *sold* to the Bank of England and sterling will automatically be back upon gold. But, so long as a country remains upon the gold standard its price level is subject, after making all the necessary allowances, to the same general influences as those operative upon the price levels of all other gold standard countries. The difference between this state of affairs and that obtaining when a country is not upon the gold standard but possesses an independent standard of its own may be expressed as follows: under the gold standard, since the rate of exchange is *not* free to vary except within very narrow limits, international parity of prices is achieved by means of gold movements and consequential changes in the price and income structure; under a paper standard, since the price and income structure is not subject to the direct influence of gold flows, international parity is achieved by means of variations in the rate of exchange. To re-state the matter somewhat differently: subject to the qualifications mentioned below, the rate of exchange between Great Britain and gold standard countries will hence-forward fluctuate according to the relative variations in gold prices and gold incomes and British paper prices and paper incomes. If prices and incomes in Great Britain remain constant, whilst gold prices and incomes rise (or, alternatively, fall), the rate of exchange between the pound sterling and francs will improve (or, alternatively, become less favourable). The more the British price structure moves in the future away from the position it had reached in September 1931 in an upward direction and the more the gold price structure moves in the opposite direction, i.e. the more sterling prices rise and gold prices fall, the less will be the number of francs bought by the pound and the more will be the number of pounds which can be bought by the franc. But the number of francs bought with paper pounds may rise, even if British prices rise, provided gold prices rise still more, whilst the number of francs bought with pounds may fall, even if British prices fall, so long as gold prices fall still more. The future exchange value of the British pound is thus not merely a function of British monetary policy, but also of the future of gold prices.

So far as other non-gold currencies are concerned, the same general rule applies. The future rate of exchange between pounds sterling and Swedish and Danish crowns will turn on the relative purchasing power in Great Britain, Sweden and Denmark respectively of the pound and the crown. The condition for stability of exchange between these currencies is that the price movements within these countries must not diverge. Since there is no longer any automatic mechanism, such as gold movements, to keep these price movements synchronized, the price movements must be managed with a view to maintaining exchange parity, otherwise fixity of exchange will be impossible.

What has been outlined above is the theory of exchange movements known to economists as the doctrine of Purchasing Power Parity. This doctrine, which leads from the relative price levels to the rate of exchange, requires, however, certain important qualifications.

The rate of exchange ruling in the market is not to be thought of as *directly* established by anything so remote as the relative price levels of two countries but is due to the supply of, and demand for, the currencies of the countries in question. The general relations between the price level and the rate of exchange are given by the fact that if, at the prevailing rate of exchange and the prevailing price levels, there is a wide disparity between the actual rate and the equilibrium rate, imports will be attracted if the rate prevailing is higher than it ought to be, whilst exports are discouraged. This will in itself tend to force the rate down towards the equilibrium or purchasing power parity rate, other things being equal. Again, if the *de facto* rate is lower than it ought to be, imports are discouraged and exports encouraged, and this will in its turn force the rate up again. It is not the fact that the exchange is below the nominal gold parity which is necessarily an encouragement to exports or to imports as the case may be, but the relation of the *de facto* rate of exchange to the equilibrium rate, as defined above. Thus, even a rate of exchange which is below the nominal gold parity may be a discouragement to exports and an encouragement to imports if, at that rate, there is 'over-valuation' in the sense that relative price levels should move the market rate downwards. But are there any valid grounds for thinking that, though an 'over-valued' or an 'under-valued' exchange itself is a cause for further movements in the market rate, tending to bring that rate more into line with the equilibrium rate, the equilibrium rate and the *de facto* rate must ultimately coincide?

The first cause of possible divergence between market rate and equilibrium or purchasing power parity rate is the influence of the anticipated future value of the currency on its present value in the exchange market. If it is believed that the future exchange value will be either lower or higher than it is now, that belief will in itself cause the present value to move downwards or upwards towards that expected future value. The most important element determining belief in this respect is the monetary policy pursued by the Government and the Central Bank. If that policy indicates a possible rise of prices in the future, the present value of the currency will fall towards what will, in the future, be the appropriate equilibrium rate; and so also for a fall of prices, which will cause exchange to rise towards the then appropriate equilibrium rate. It is altogether impossible to eliminate anticipation, and thus the coincidence of market and equilibrium rate can never, in all probability, be a perfect one.

In the second place, there are conceivable conditions in which the purchasing power parity rate is itself not the true equilibrium rate, so that there may be divergence between the *de facto* rate, the true equilibrium rate, and the purchasing power parity rate. In the case of two gold standard countries, gold flows take place until the price and income structure is such that the balance of payments is adjusted by means of the flow of goods. If one of these gold standard countries desires the products of the other more urgently than its own products are desired in their turn, it will go on losing gold until its own price and income structure has fallen to a sufficiently low level to force a demand for its goods, i.e. its price level will be lower than it would have been if its goods had been in greater demand. Under a paper standard the price and income structure is not *directly* affected, except in so far as goods imported must be sold at a price which covers the cost of exchange; if one of the trading countries desires the product of the other more urgently than its own products are desired, the method of adjustment will be a fall in the rate of exchange to an *abnormal* level, lower than is justified by comparative prices, in order both to stimulate an additional demand for its own products and to cut off part of its own demand for foreign products. An alteration in the intensity of a country's demand for foreign products may therefore make the true equilibrium rate of exchange different from (and lower or higher than) the purchasing power parity rate. But there still remains the possibility that there will be lack of coincidence between the actual market rate and the true equilibrium rate: the market rate may still be too high or too low in comparison to that true equilibrium rate.

The doctrine of purchasing power parity is without doubt essential to an understanding of fundamental conditions: in sum, it merely expresses the truth that in a money economy the relative values of different monetary units must bear some relation to their relative purchasing powers, in other words to their command over goods and services. If one proceeds, however, to ask how far the doctrine is directly of use in explaining all the confused phenomena of the last few years, then it must be admitted that certain qualifications which have already been stated in general terms have come to possess a significance which requires explicit statement. What we have in fact now to investigate is the influence exerted, at a time of grave international depression, by the phenomena of over-valued and under-valued currencies, when they are accompanied, as they have been in recent years, not only by deliberately induced changes in the relative intensities of demand for the products of particular countries *inter se* but by the introduction of artificial methods of control over capital movements and over fluctuations in the rates of exchange themselves. Let us put these issues as concretely as possible. Great Britain's departure from the gold standard is not the only factor which has had a bearing on the course of events since 1931. At that time the world depression was already severe, and the abandonment of gold by a world power at such a time might well produce consequences different from those which might have been the result if Great Britain had abandoned gold whilst general conditions were good. Since 1931 many countries have abandoned gold; a whole series of quota and licence restrictions as well as of additional tariff rates have come into existence: capital movements and interest payments have been greatly impeded by moratoria and exchange controls; finally, in 1932 Great Britain created an Exchange Equalization Fund to eliminate minor exchange fluctuations, and her example was followed by the U.S.A. in 1934. It is obvious that to estimate the direct effect of Great Britain's abandonment of gold, upon herself and the rest of the world, is an exceedingly difficult task, for, apart from the difficulty of disentangling the effects of any one cause, the initiating factors have in part stood in the relation of cause and effect to one another. Thus the abandonment of gold by Great Britain led to the abandonment of the gold standard by the Scandinavian countries and by some of the countries of the British Empire, and Japan followed soon after. In the ultimate analysis it may be said that even the temporary abandonment of gold by the U.S.A. is psychologically connected with the British experiment. The abandonment of gold, the introduction of exchange controls, tariffs and quotas, etc., constitute an organic complex of events, and it is almost, if not quite, impossible to separate the respective consequences of all these measures. It may be possible to do something analytically, but it is in my judgment impossible to *prove* one's analysis by an appeal to positive fact: the situation is too complicated.

Let us first investigate the effects to be expected from the over-valuation or under-valuation of the pound sterling. In addition to the element of anticipation already alluded to, the pound has been subject to the influence of capital movements from time to time. The fear that the U.S.A. might be driven off the gold standard before that event actually happened, the fear that the dollar might fall sharply after gold had actually been abandoned, and doubts as to the fortune of the gold standard in the Gold Bloc countries resulted in an inflow of funds into Great Britain—a movement which, unless counteracted, might easily raise the level of sterling temporarily above the true equilibrium point. The necessity to buy foreign currencies to meet accruing foreign indebtedness (such, for example, as that incurred in the summer of 1931 in order to defend the pound) or to meet the demand for repayment of balances held in London, if the foreign holders thought the immediate outlook for sterling unfavourable, would have the opposite effect: it would help to drive sterling below the equilibrium point, considered from the standpoint of relative prices in both cases. An over-valued pound would have the effect, given a certain level of prices abroad, of causing the prices of imports here to rise more than would otherwise be the case, and of checking exports, for, given a certain level of sterling prices, British exports would *pro tanto* cost the foreigner more.

These effects would, however, be self-corrective, other things being equal (that is, assuming that a fall in sterling did not encourage speculative sales or a rise encourage speculative purchases or, in either case, movements of balances). Rising sterling prices for imports would cause them to decrease, thus reducing the demand for foreign remittance: on the other hand rising prices to the foreigner would cause him to cut down his consumption of British goods, thus checking the rise in sterling.

In general one would expect that, in so far as British prices were to rise as a consequence of exchange rates with foreign countries being above what they were before (in terms of sterling) or below what they were before (in terms of foreign currencies), the rise in the cost of imports *per se* would be greater absolutely than the rise of prices in general of those goods for the manufacture of which these imports were required, since domestic costs, which need not alter directly at all, merely in consequence of a fall in exchange, are a larger proportion of the total cost of such manufactured goods. It is also obvious that those goods which were absolutely necessary to us would rise most in price, whilst things which could be replaced, either by less expensive (even if less suitable) substitutes, or by commodities of home origin, are not at all, or only indirectly, affected by the influences exerted by the exchange. In the case of Great Britain, the great emporium for overseas products and a large importer for foodstuffs, these considerations are more than usually significant, especially at a time of agricultural depression, when unsold stocks are pressing upon the market in any case. For sales in sterling may have the direct result of depressing the local price level of agricultural produce. The very fact that the pound falls in value in terms of the local currency implies a unit fall in the value of produce sold in the British market, unless sterling prices can be made to rise in exact correspondence to the fall in exchange. If the demand for overseas supplies of foodstuffs and raw materials, however, is such that the demand falls off if the price goes up, it is probable that foreign sellers, rather than lose their market, will submit to a reduction of price, in terms of the local currency. The only way of avoiding such a loss is to abandon the gold standard, so that the local currency continues to be worth as much as before in terms of sterling. In so far as local prices of exportable products remain unchanged, and the local currency now varies in terms of gold as sterling varies, what in fact has happened is that the gold value of the local products has fallen. This fall in the gold value enables local producers to compete more successfully, both in the British markets and in neutral markets, with products of a similar kind coming from countries still upon the gold standard, and with goods coming from gold standard countries for which, at the new level of prices, goods coming from paper standard countries are more or less efficient substitutes. In this way the abandonment of the gold standard by a single important country acting as the main source of demand for competitively produced raw materials may exert an important influence, not only upon the course of currency policy in many parts of the world, but upon the general level of world prices for foodstuffs and raw materials. What has already been said does not, however, exhaust all the possibilities. Maintaining parity with sterling is not the only possibility open to raw material producing countries; they may choose to see sterling going to a premium in terms of the local currency. In that case the money incomes derived by exporters from the sales of local produce to Great Britain expand in terms of the local currency and they may be thereby encouraged to push their sales. The effect may then be to cause not only additional pressure upon producers in gold standard countries—for they cannot sell their products at sterling prices which are above the competitive level—but also to produce an actual fall in the level of sterling prices for the commodities in question: the market may be glutted in consequence of the efforts of local exporters to expand aggregate money receipts in terms of local currency to a maximum, but in reality overshooting the optimum point. A fall in sterling prices will, in these circumstances, be accompanied by a fall in local incomes and a fall in the unit prices of local produce, unless the exchange on sterling is allowed to fall still further.

These influences on the price level of internationally traded goods (and indirectly upon domestic prices) may be reinforced or counter-checked by the effects produced by tariff legislation, quota restrictions, and the control of the market for capital loans and for foreign exchange itself. The general effect of a tariff rate is to check imports and so to raise the price level of the goods affected: at the same time by checking imports it may have some effect upon the rate of exchange itself, so that the net result may be that the cost of an imported commodity plus duty but with a somewhat higher rate of exchange may not differ significantly from the cost of a similar article imported duty free but at a somewhat lower rate of exchange. A quota which limits the total amount to be imported works in the same direction: so far as the importing country is concerned, the question of whether prices will or will not rise depends upon the relative importance of the effect upon the rate of exchange, the net decline in quantities imported and the result of the decline upon local demand. But the issue is not disposed of by considering merely these repercussions: one must also take into account what may happen in the exporting area. Tariffs and quotas alike, in so far as they succeed in checking imports, must reduce unit prices of the commodities formerly exported unless alternative sources of demand are available or output is cut down. In order to avoid the resulting loss of receipts, the imposition of a tariff rate or a quota may be met by raising the value of sterling in terms of the local currency: tariff manipulation is followed by currency depreciation which in its turn may be followed by still further quota restrictions and tariff impositions. At a time of grave international depression, and taking into account the inelastic character of agricultural production, it is difficult to escape the general conclusion that tariffs and quotas imposed with the idea, *inter alia*, of protecting rates of exchange, have a seriously deflationary effect upon the price level of international raw materials.

Restrictions upon the free movement of capital and the free purchase and sale of foreign exchange must obviously work in the same direction. The agricultural countries of the world notoriously suffer more from depression than industrial states, in the sense that their aggregate income varies more abruptly between periods of good and bad trade. But these countries are all debtor States, owing money to the more 'advanced' areas. To pay interest and amortization upon debts fixed in terms of money involves the export of greater real quantities of goods in times of bad trade. One way of avoiding some of the pressure so induced is to borrow during the period of depression in order to repay when times are better. This is difficult enough in any case owing to the natural disinclination of the investor to take up the securities of countries which are known to be doing badly; but, if the hesitancies of the investor are reinforced by the restrictions imposed by Governments, 'distress borrowing' becomes impossible. If at the same time the traditional lending areas impose new or additional duties on imports, the task of the agricultural countries becomes an impossible one—the very effort to pay their debts, by increasing the quantum of their exports, brings down upon them a new series of penalties. Hence they default or depreciate their currencies, or do both these things together. This in its turn may result in a new series of penalties being imposed. The general effect is deflationary. Again, if such countries are not allowed to use freely such assets in the way of foreign exchange as they may have accumulated in the past the result must be to increase the pressure on current exports and to cause them to be offered at lower prices.

Before any final summing up can be attempted it is necessary to consider the position, not only from the standpoint of the internal price level in Great Britain or of countries exporting to Great Britain, but also from the standpoint of countries buying from Great Britain, or in competition with her in neutral markets. A fall in the external value of the pound, in so far as it merely compensates for the higher level of money costs inside the country, does nothing more than restore Great Britain's competitive position to what it would have been if the gold standard had been restored at a lower gold content, or had not been restored at all, in 1925. The extent to which the pound must fall in order to effect this depends on the actual level of relative costs at any time and cannot be measured by what it was at some time in the past. Costs do not remain constant over time. A rise in wage-rates, induced by a rise in the cost of living due to the higher cost of imported goods, would at once affect the equilibrium position. In so far as the pound was over-valued before the abandonment of gold by some 10 per cent, a fall in the external value of the pound by 10 per cent does not give Great Britain any special advantage, but merely removes a disadvantage. If the exchange, however, for any reason falls by more than is required to offset a higher cost structure, that is, if the pound is under-valued, Great Britain enjoys a special, though it may be merely a temporary, export bonus. She can for the moment under-sell industrial rivals, or, if a group of manufacturers are selling a monopolized commodity at fixed prices in foreign currency, they obtain a larger monopoly profit. In a depressed world the effect of under-valuation and the special stimulus to exports which it affords is to cause additional difficulties to countries with a fixed exchange, which they can try to meet either by reducing costs, imposing additional duties, or abandoning gold themselves. The most important case in which this alternative was adopted was that of Japan, for Japan is in some important respects more directly in competition with Great Britain than is the U.S.A., though in the case of the United States also the temporary abandonment of gold and the considerable under-valuation which accompanied this step increased the competitive zone, that is, the range of commodities exportable from America in competition with British exports.

There can, I think, be little doubt that Great Britain's departure from the gold standard had consequences, both inside and outside the country, which were not anticipated at the time. So far as the internal situation is concerned, the fact that Great Britain's example encouraged many important suppliers of foodstuffs and raw materials to follow her, added to the circumstance that in a nationalistic, tariff-ridden world this country was a quasi-monopolistic buyer, resulted in a smaller rise of prices, direct and indirect, than most instructed persons would have thought possible in 1931. On the other hand, the high hopes entertained that Great

Britain's exports would be greatly stimulated have hardly been borne out by facts. The special disadvantage of an (uncompensated) higher cost structure has indeed disappeared, but the cumulative effects of continued world depression, tariffs and quotas, and imitation by other industrial competitors, especially Japan, has severely limited the direct gain to this country. Since there can hardly be any doubt that the depression has been prolonged by the uncertainties and difficulties caused by the interferences with the free flow of international trade, there are no indirect gains. At best it might be argued that Great Britain has been able to snatch a rather larger share of a greatly shrunken aggregate: against this possible advantage must be set the fact that Great Britain's action was a considerable factor in producing that complex of governmental actions which has impeded recovery, even though at the moment of writing the outlook is undoubtedly much more cheerful than it has been for a long time past.[1]

PART II: A STATISTICAL SURVEY

IN THIS section the attempt is made to depict the general course of development in this country since September 18th 1931. Thus its emphasis is primarily upon internal changes: upon the movements of exchange and prices, production, and the volume of employment. But in one sense it may be said that the most important influence exerted by Great Britain's departure from gold was not upon internal economic conditions at all (the magnitude of that influence quantitatively being in any case, as already pointed out, an extremely difficult thing to measure) but upon the course of currency policy in other parts of the world, both within and without the

[1] May 1934.

British Empire. Even before Great Britain's defection, the position of the gold standard had become imperilled by the course of the depression: there can be very little doubt, however, that the example of Great Britain became highly infectious. This was so, not only because abandonment of gold here inflicted a serious blow upon the prestige of the gold standard itself and made other countries less anxious to sustain the sacrifices which retention of the old parities with gold might seem to involve: reasons more directly connected with the specific situation of the various countries concerned can be advanced as well. The fundamental factor is the dependence of many countries, both overseas and in Europe, upon the British domestic market: this is a consideration of great importance in the case of Scandinavia as well as of New Zealand and the raw material areas generally. In other cases, it was not so much dependence on the British domestic market which proved decisive as fear that a falling pound sterling would increase Great Britain's competitive position, and, in the case of Japan, this consideration was no doubt of overwhelming importance. Once a large part of the world was off gold, however, the pressure upon those countries still upon gold increased. Thus Great Britain's action, though it did not by any means initiate the flight from gold, very greatly strengthened the tendencies already present. Norway, Sweden, and Egypt suspended gold payments on September 27th 1931; Denmark on the 28th; Finland and Northern and Southern Rhodesia suspended on October 12th; whilst Canada officially followed on October 19th. India, because it was associated with sterling, automatically 'went off' gold when Great Britain did; the Australasian Dominions were already off gold. Japan left the gold standard on December 13th 1931, Siam in May 1932, and South Africa on December 13th

1932. All these changes can be directly associated with the changes in the monetary status of this country. America's defection, which will be separately dealt with in the next chapter, presents special problems of its own.

1. *The Course of Prices and of the Exchange*

The general course of prices and of the gold exchanges can be followed from the accompanying Table I and Chart No. 1.[1] Up to March 1933 the United States was upon the gold standard; up to that date, therefore, the 'sterling price of gold' measures also the premium, in terms of sterling, upon the American gold dollar. After that date, the sterling cost of acquiring dollars fell rapidly until a period of comparative stability was reached in the early part of 1934—one of the direct consequences of the devaluation of the dollar through the Gold Reserve Act of 1934.

(1) Before dealing with the minor details of these movements it is desirable to draw attention to the most conspicuous feature clearly shown by the chart. The rise in the price of gold in terms of sterling has far outstripped the rise in the sterling price of commodities, though sterling primary prices have been more affected, at times considerably more affected, than sterling prices, as measured through the 'Complete Index'. It does not follow, of course, that because gold rises by a given percentage in terms of sterling that prices, even of imported commodities, must rise by a similar percentage, for gold prices may have fallen, and it will be seen that until March 1933 the movement of gold prices is at times almost the inverse of the movement of the premium upon gold in terms of sterling: so that fluctuations of

[1] Reproduced here by permission of the Editor of *The Economist.*

Date	British Complete Inde (Sterling)	Products.		Sterling Price of Gold	Irving Fish U.S.A.	Statistiqu Générale France	Milan Cham of Commer Italy	Statistisch Reichsam Germany
		British (Sterling)	American (Dollars)					
1931								
Sept. 30th	107·8	112·0	94·7	123·9	98·7	96·9	98·8	98·9
Oct. 28th	108·4	114·4	101·4	124·5	99·3	95·6	99·9	98·7
Nov. 28th	109·1	114·8	98·0	131·6	98·3	94·2	98·8	97·6
Dec. 30th	108·9	117·1	94·4	142·0	96·1	93·4	96·9	94·6
1932								
Jan. 27th	108·3	115·7	93·8	140·9	93·5	93·6	95·8	91·6
Feb. 24th	110·9	120·9	89·6	139·8	92·4	95·1	97·2	92·0
Mar. 22nd	108·1	111·9	86·5	133·1	91·5	96·3	97·0	91·4
Apr. 20th	103·8	105·4	83·6	129·5	89·6	97·0	95·3	90·3
June 1st	100·2	101·0	79·8	132·7	87·3	94·0	91·7	88·5
June 29th	97·4	99·3	80·5	135·0	86·4	91·5	89·5	88·1
July 27th	99·5	103·5	84·1	136·9	88·3	91·3	88·5	88·1
Aug. 24th	102·5	111·8	89·3	140·0	89·8	89·0	89·3	87·1
Sept. 21st	106·0	117·4	89·6	139·9	90·5	89·7	91·2	87·1
Oct. 19th	103·1	112·3	84·0	143·8	88·6	88·8	92·7	86·8
Nov. 30th	103·1	112·3	77·7	153·8	87·3	88·4	91·4	85·2
Dec. 28th	101·2	109·3	76·9	145·6	83·5	88·1	90·9	84·2
1933								
Jan. 28th	101·3	107·7	78·0	142·6	80·5	88·1	90·2	83·8
Feb. 22nd	99·5	104·2	76·9	143·2	79·9	88·1	88·7	84·3
Mar. 22nd	99·0	104·0	80·1	142·1	82·1	87·2	87·5	83·4
Apr. 19th	98·7	104·6	88·7	141·4	82·8	87·5	86·2	83·4
May 31st	105·3	116·3	108·5	145·8	90·0	87·2	86·6	84·9
June 28th	107·6	118·2	117·4	144·0	94·4	89·5	87·2	85·6
July 26th	108·1	120·6	124·7	145·7	100·9	89·7	86·2	86·6
Aug. 23rd	107·9	116·9	119·0	147·6	102·1	89·5	86·2	86·6
Sept. 20th	108·1	116·9	120·7	157·4	103·7	87·5	85·8	87·5
Oct. 18th	106·4	112·8	109·1	155·4	103·7	87·5	84·6	88·1
Nov. 29th	104·4	114·7	117·2	147·7	103·5	86·8	84·5	88·2
Dec. 13th	105·3	114·8	117·0	148·4	104·4	87·2	84·5	88·4
1934								
Jan. 31st	108·8	118·0	124·8	156·7	105·6	87·2	84·4	88·5
Feb. 28th	109·1	121·3	128·0	161·3	107·9	86·1	84·1	88·0
Mar. 28th	108·3	121·4	127·5	160·4	107·3	85·9	84·2	88·1
Apr. 25th	108·2	119·8	125·3	159·5	106·0	85·4	83·2	87·7
May 23rd	108·2	121·4	128·8	160·7	109·5	84·7	83·9	88·5
June 6th	108·2	122·3	134·4	162·3	110·1	84·1	83·8	88·9
June 20th	108·1	123·4	133·9	162·3	113·1	82·7	83·9	89·6
July 4th	107·7	123·2	[illegible]	161·7	[illegible]	[illegible]*	[illegible]*	[illegible]

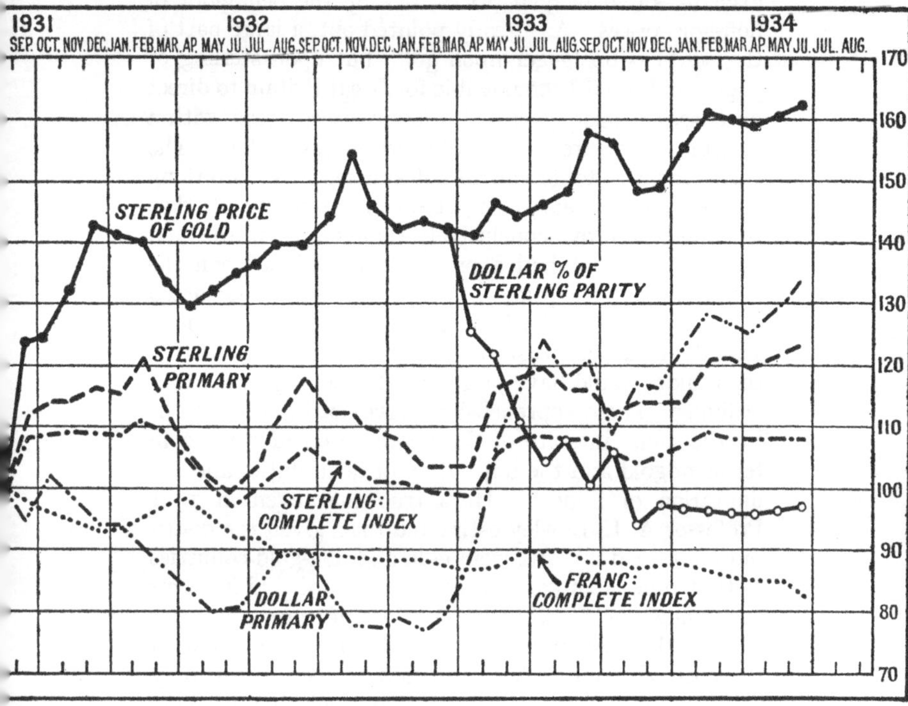

(September 18th 1931 = 100)

-·-·- Sterling Wholesale Prices (all commodities)
— — Sterling Wholesale Prices (primary commodities)
··-··- American (dollar) Wholesale Prices (primary commodities)
·········· French (franc) Wholesale Prices
—●—●— Sterling Price of Gold
—○—○— Value of dollar in sterling as percentage of parity

sterling import prices represent the combined results of two contradictory trends. Moreover, sterling import prices are affected, not only by the movement of the exchanges and of gold prices, but by the behaviour of non-gold prices. As already pointed out, a large part of the world is no longer upon gold, but upon sterling or paper, and it has been possible for Great Britain to direct purchases to such (relatively) lower priced areas, with a resultant pressure upon gold prices themselves. The chart and the table cannot, of course, prove anything whatsoever as regards the chain of causation: all that they do is to prove conclusively that the rise in the gold premium has not had a proportionate effect upon the course of domestic prices. When Great Britain departed from the gold standard there was some apprehension—shared in part at least by the writer—that the action then taken would have pronounced effects upon the cost of living. These apprehensions have not been borne out by the facts, in spite of the depreciation of sterling in terms of gold and the imposition of tariff duties and the limitation of imports. It is true that even in 1931 Professor A. L. Bowley estimated that, given the distribution of food imports from gold and non-gold countries at that time, a 25 per cent appreciation of gold in terms of sterling would involve an increase of some 4 per cent only in the cost of living, since, of the 60 per cent of the cost of living index composed of food items, only half was attributable to imports, and only half of these again were imported from gold standard countries.[1] The gold premium has, however, since risen to some 60 per cent and meanwhile the cost of living index has actually fallen from a monthly average (Base: July 1914 = 100) of 147 in 1931 to 143 in 1932 and 1933 to 138 in May

[1] *London and Cambridge Economic Service Bulletin*, No. 10, Vol. IX, p. 307.

1934. Such results could certainly not have been anticipated on *a priori* grounds.

(2) Turning now to the fluctuations in the various series, it will be seen that the sterling price of gold, whilst tending to move constantly upwards, displays a strong wave-like movement. In each of the years 1931, 1932, and 1933, there is a peak in the autumn and a minimum in the spring: in 1933, however, there is also a minimum in the autumn after the peak, whilst a new maximum was attained in February of 1934—these latter phenomena being no doubt associated with the vagaries of American currency policy, to be discussed in the next chapter. It will be noted, too, that the fluctuations in the course of sterling primary prices accompany the movements of the exchanges fairly closely, though with a tendency to lag somewhat behind in the earlier years and to be less pronounced in the later years. The complete index of sterling prices, though much less sensitive, also tends to move with the curve representing the premium on gold. The divorce between the movements in the gold premium and the price-curves in the later period (after the beginning of 1933) is again to be associated with the abandonment of the gold standard by the U.S.A.

(3) The magnitude of the fluctuations in the price curves is, as already suggested, a function not only of the movements of the gold or other exchanges, but also of overseas prices. The chart brings out very clearly the rather astonishing fact that the level of sterling primary prices in the early period of depreciation attained a maximum (120) which was not reached again till the middle of July 1933, though the trend of the gold premium had been rising. This second peak is clearly associated with the uprush of American primary prices in the spring of 1933, under the combined influence of a

falling dollar, the Agricultural Adjustment Act, and widespread speculation in commodities. Whilst, at the earlier date, falling prices in the U.S.A. tended to neutralize the sharp rise in the premium, at the second date rising American prices were tending to neutralize the effect of a rapidly depreciating dollar.

This rapid survey leaves open the question of the exact extent to which from time to time the pound sterling has been over-valued or under-valued in terms of other currencies. That the pound should have been worth more in terms of dollars, until America herself abandoned gold, is *a priori* probable when the movements of exchange are compared with the movements of price. Moreover, the question whether such over-valuation or under-valuation as exists has been influenced by monetary or governmental policy is also one of considerable significance. Both these issues will be examined in a separate section.

2. *The Course of Production and of Employment*

Economic activity in Great Britain is more closely related to the international economic order than in any other leading industrial country. This is not entirely due to the magnitude of the export industries and the possession of a large mercantile marine: nor is it due only to the direct influence exerted by capital exports and the financial activities of the City of London as the centre of the world's international clearing system. These factors affect the economic situation of Great Britain directly, but they also affect it indirectly, in the sense that a vast mass of derived employment exists which fluctuates with the income earned through the activities so far mentioned. It follows from this that the British economy ought to be very profoundly influenced by so far-reaching an event as the departure from the gold standard.

As already pointed out, the abandonment of gold might be expected to assist the position of this country by stimulating exports (through the closer adjustment of nominal costs to the outside price level) and by checking imports. But it might also have indirect (though favourable) repercussions of a psychological nature. Certainty is never as deterrent in economic matters, even though the certainty be bad, as fear of the unknown. Consequently, abandoning gold may have stimulated industrial activity, not because the technical features of the situation were profoundly altered thereby, but because it marked the end of a long-drawn crisis. The gold standard had been made responsible in the eyes of the public for much of the so-called 'depression' of the period 1925–30 and was consequently very unpopular. The mere fact that it no longer existed might therefore have acted as a psychological stimulant. Moreover, the public had been taught in the summer of 1931 to expect unfavourable results from the abandonment of gold: it experienced a distinct sense of relief when these failed to show themselves immediately, in any obvious way—for the chain of causation which leads from the abandonment of gold to an intensification of the world crisis, via competitive exchange depreciation and the whole apparatus of governmental interference with the free flow of capital and goods is by no means an obvious one —and this sense of relief may again have helped to restore confidence. Thus the indirect consequences of the abandonment of gold might well prove more important than the direct, in the long run. Dethroning gold may have helped recovery merely because the public had been taught to expect miracles if gold were dethroned. Further, it has to be remembered that almost

TABLE II

INDICES OF PRODUCTION AND OF BUSINESS ACTIVITY

(A) London and Cambridge Economic Service Quarterly Index of Production

Average 1924 = 100

	1929	1930	1931	1932	1933	1934
1st Quarter	108·3	109·6	85·1	91·3	88·0	102·2
2nd Quarter	111·0	100·9	80·6	83·2	88·8	
3rd Quarter	108·2	90·7	81·1	77·8	87·9	
4th Quarter	114·8	92·7	90·5	87·2	97·4	

(B) 'The Economist' Index of Business Activity Three Months' Moving Average †

1924 = 100

	1929	1930	1931	1932	1933	1934
January .	106·6	111·2	100·4	94·3	96·5	105·9
February .	106·4	110·5	98·9	94·9	96·6	107·4
March .	107·6	110·6	97·8	95·5	96·6	109·1
April . .	108·1	110·0	97·2	96·6	96·6	108·6*
May . .	109·7	109·3	97·3	95·8	97·8	107·4*
June . .	110·2	107·9	97·5	96·5	98·3	
July . .	110·2	105·5	98·1	95·6	99·6	
August .	111·0	104·0	97·7	95·9	101·1	
September	111·4	103·4	96·1	94·6	102·2	
October .	110·7	103·5	94·1	94·9	102·5	
November.	110·8	102·5	93·7	95·3	102·7	
December .	110·6	101·7	93·9	96·7	102·9	

* Provisional. † Partly corrected for seasonal variations.

(C) Board of Trade Index of Industrial Production

Base 1924 = 100

	1929	1930	1931	1932	1933	1934
1st Quarter	110·4	111·0	95·0	94·3	94·8	108·4
2nd Quarter	111·9	103·1	91·9	87·3	96·7	
3rd Quarter	110·6	99·5	89·3	95·0	96·8	
4th Quarter	113·5	99·0	96·8	94·8	105·0	

CHART No. 2

INDICES OF PRODUCTION

(1924 = 100)

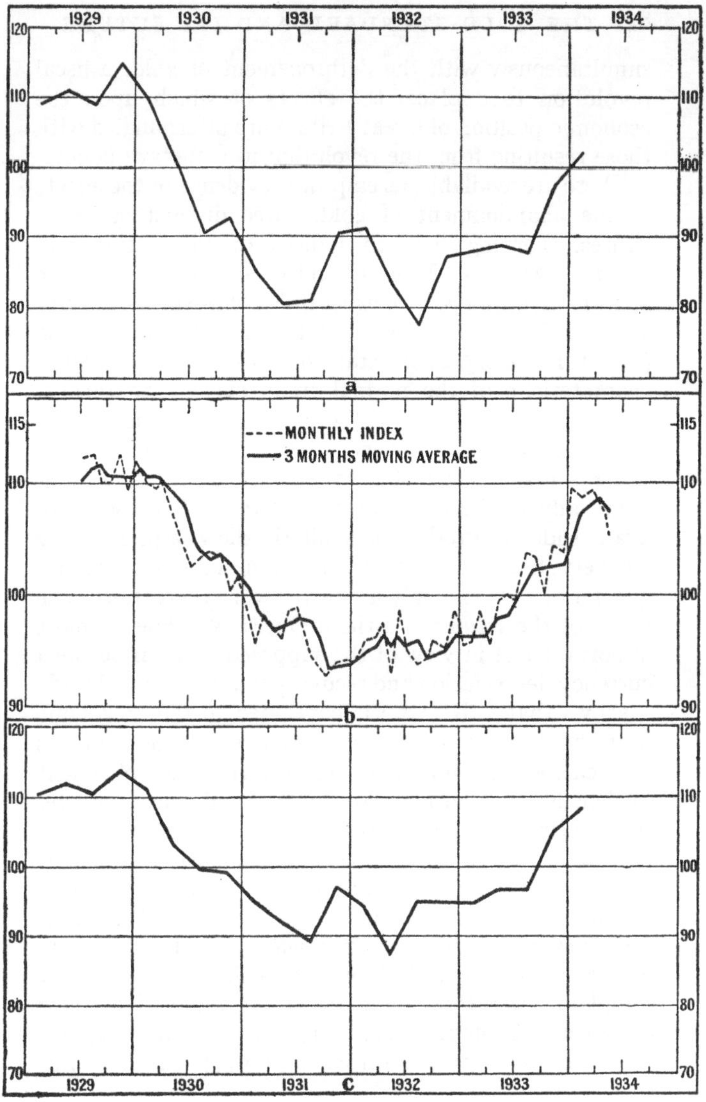

(*a*) London and Cambridge Quarterly Index of Production
(*b*) *The Economist* Index of Business Activity
(*c*) Board of Trade Index of Industrial Production

simultaneously with the dethronement of gold, a fiscal revolution took place, the effects of which upon the economic position of Great Britain are intermingled with those resulting from the revolution in monetary policy.

There are available, as empirical evidence of the effects of the abandonment of gold, three distinct series of figures. Turning first to indices of Productive and Business Activity (Table II and Chart No. 2) it will be seen that whilst *The Economist* Index of Business Activity shows a distinct turning point towards the end of 1931 (whilst revealing in general the wave-like appearance characteristic of the normal trade cycle), the turning point in the London and Cambridge Economic Service Index, after some recovery in the last quarter of 1931 and the first quarter of 1932, reaches an absolute minimum only in the third quarter of 1932. The Board of Trade Index of Production similarly shows a preliminary recovery, but reaches an absolute minimum in the second quarter of 1932 and only a slow recovery thereafter. The index of the *volume* of British Overseas Trade—a most important test in view of the supposed relation between currency depreciation and recovery in international trade—shows that U.K. exports continued to fall in volume until the third quarter of 1932, a quarter in which imports also reached their minimum (Table III). Unemployment (which, it must be pointed out, was influenced also by the results of the Economy Campaign) fell seasonally in December 1931, but rose almost continuously throughout the first half of 1932 and only began to show a definitely declining trend from the middle of 1933 (*vide* Table IV). This is especially so as regards *male* unemployment. As regards prices, Table I above shows that *The Economist* complete index rose some 10 per cent, then fell below the level of September 18th 1931 by June of 1932, was below the base level again early in 1933, and has only shown a somewhat hesitating upward movement ever since. Other indices also reveal a sharp upward turn immediately after the abandonment of gold, a collapse later and a marked tendency to rise recently.

The evidence that the abandonment of the gold standard marks the turning point in the great depression is thus far from conclusive. It might perhaps be contended that the continuance of adverse conditions elsewhere (the Gold Bloc countries, the United States) is negative evidence of the wisdom of the step taken in 1931. But this argument assumes that our action did not *intensify* adverse conditions elsewhere, so that all that can be urged is that we snatched a temporary advantage at the expense of others. This counter-argument cannot be proved by an appeal to statistics, any more than the contention against which it is directed. There is some evidence that the abandonment of gold and the sharp depreciation of the exchanges had certain direct beneficial reactions in the short run which were dissipated as time went on, and had more lasting effects upon psychology and the state of public confidence. More than this cannot be said, in the considered judgment of the writer.

3. *The Under-valuation of the Pound and the Exchange Equalization Fund*

The efficacy of a falling exchange, as an instrument of competition, turns largely upon whether it results in over-valuation or under-valuation of the currency. It becomes important to inquire what the position of sterling has been in recent years: the causes which may have produced over-valuation or under-valuation have already been sufficiently discussed.

TABLE III

VOLUME OF BRITISH OVERSEAS TRADE

1930 = 100

	1931		1932		1933		1934	
	Total Imports	U.K. Exports	Total Imports	U.K. Exports	Total Imports	U.K. Exports	Total Imports	U Ex
1st Quarter .	95·2	77·7	95·0	76·9	87·0	76·5	96·5	8
2nd Quarter .	97·6	74·0	85·7	78·8	88·0	73·9	—	–
3rd Quarter .	99·2	74·4	85·0	71·8	89·8	79·2	—	–
4th Quarter .	117·3	78·8	94·9	79·9	97·8	84·1	—	–

1924: Total Imports, 91·6; Exports U.K. Produce, 116·2

TABLE IV

THE COURSE OF UNEMPLOYMENT

ercentages of Insured Persons Recorded as Unemployed : Great Britain and Northern Ireland

	1929			1930			1931			1932			1933		
	Males	Fe-males	Total	Males	Fe-males	Total	Males	Fe-males	Total	Males	Fe-males	Total	Males	Fe-males	Tc
	13·6	8·3	12·2	13·3	10·2	12·4	21·7	19·5	21·1	24·8	15·5	22·2	26·3	14·2	2
	13·7	7·7	12·1	13·7	11·0	12·9	22·2	19·2	21·3	24·7	14·4	21·9	25·9	14·0	2
ch	11·2	6·7	10·0	14·2	12·4	13·7	22·2	17·9	21·0	23·8	12·8	20·8	25·1	13·7	2
l	11·0	6·7	9·8	14·6	13·3	14·2	21·5	17·5	20·4	24·4	13·0	21·3	24·3	13·2	2
	10·9	6·6	9·7	15·2	14·4	15·0	21·4	17·4	20·3	25·0	14·2	22·0	23·6	12·0	2
	10·8	6·6	9·6	15·6	14·8	15·4	22·5	17·8	21·2	25·3	13·8	22·2	22·7	10·8	1
	10·8	6·9	9·7	17·0	15·8	16·7	23·1	18·9	21·9	26·0	14·4	22·8	22·7	10·9	1
	10·8	7·4	9·9	17·2	16·4	17·0	23·0	19·3	21·9	26·2	14·5	23·0	22·4	10·5	1
	10·9	7·2	9·9	17·8	16·7	17·5	23·5	19·6	22·4	26·2	13·9	22·8	21·6	10·0	1
	11·4	7·4	10·3	19·2	16·6	18·5	23·4	17·3	21·7	25·5	12·4	21·9	21·4	9·5	1
	12·0	7·8	10·9	19·6	17·0	18·9	23·4	15·7	21·2	25·7	12·9	22·2	21·1	9·4	1
	12·2	7·9	11·0	20·4	18·5	19·9	22·9	14·9	20·7	25·1	12·5	21·6	20·8	9·0	1

Before Great Britain's departure from the gold standard, it was generally assumed in expert circles that *some* over-valuation of the pound existed. The following Chart and Tables take account of this prevailing impression, in that they attempt to estimate the situation on the assumptions (1) that the pound was at a true par with the American dollar on the basis of a dollar-sterling rate of $4·86 to the pound, (2) that the true parity was some 10 per cent lower than this, i.e. the 'equilibrium' rate should have been, not $4·86, but $4·40 to the pound. A comparison is made on the basis of American and British wholesale prices, and upon the basis of American and British cost of living indices. The numerical results are given in Table V, but in order to obtain an easier oversight Chart No. 3 and Table VI record the coefficient of deviation between the actual rate ruling at any period and the calculated purchasing power parity rate. If these two rates coincide, the result equals 100. If the actual rate is lower than it ought to be in comparison with the purchasing power parity rate, the result exceeds 100 and the deviation measures the degree of under-valuation. If the result is less than 100, the pound is over-valued in terms of the dollar, or, what comes to the same thing, the dollar is under-valued in terms of the pound.

Whilst the chart is useful as showing the directions of change over the three years 1931–3, it does not, of course, prove the absolute magnitude of the degree of over-valuation or under-valuation actually present during those years; all it does is to illustrate and confirm the general impression that the pound was over-valued before gold was abandoned and that this over-valuation gave place to under-valuation thereafter. The chart shows very clearly the fundamental changes wrought in the situation by the departure of the U.S.A. from the gold standard in December 1933, and shows also what an immediate effect was produced by the movements of funds in the early part of 1932, when sterling rose from \$3·430 in January to a maximum of \$3·752 in April. By the end of 1933 the under-valuation of the pound was some 10 per cent on the most favourable supposition, and may have been as much as 20 per cent over-valued—in terms, of course, of the American dollar—on the assumption that \$4·40 was the true equilibrium rate and the cost of living relatives the proper measuring rod. At any rate, it is clear that the change in American currency policy very profoundly modified the competitive situation of sterling: the outcome must largely depend upon the course of prices in the U.S.A. as well as in this country.

The course of exchange during the last three years has not been entirely left to the free play of 'market prices', numerous as these are in themselves. Almost from the very beginning of the era of the paper standard, the movement of the rate has been subject to official intervention[1]—first by the Bank of England acting on its own account, and later by the Bank of England acting on behalf of the Exchange Equalization Account, created by authority of the Finance Act of 1932. Originally the amount of the Exchange Fund was fixed at £150 millions, but was raised to £350 millions by the Finance Act of 1933; and, by the original legislation on the subject, 'the Treasury may cause any funds in the Account to be invested in securities or in the purchase of gold as they think best adapted for checking undue fluctuations in the exchange value of sterling'. For this purpose the

[1] The following paragraphs largely repeat what I have already written on this subject in the Introduction to the second edition of this book. For a very useful and more elaborate inquiry cf. N. F. Hall, *The British Exchange Equalization Account*, published as a supplement to *The Economist* of May 5th 1934.

TABLE

OVER-VALUATION AND UNDER-

Date		British Wholesale Prices, Bd. of Trade General	American Wholesale Prices	Cost of Living	
				British	American
1924	.	100	100	100	100
1931	Jan.	64·3	80·0	87	88
	Feb.	63·9	78·5	86	87·5
	March	63·7	77·5	84	87
	April	63·6	76·0	84	85·5
	May	62·8	74·5	83	84·5
	June	62·1	73·5	84	84·5
	July	61·5	73·5	83	84·5
	Aug.	59·9	73·5	83	84
	Sept.	59·7	72·5	83	83·5
	Oct.	62·8	71·5	83·5	82·5
	Nov.	64·0	71·5	84·5	82
	Dec.	63·7	70·0	84	80
1932	Jan.	63·4	68·5	84	79
	Feb.	63·4	67·5	83·5	78·5
	March	63·0	67·5	82·5	77·5
	April	61·6	67·0	81·5	76·5
	May	60·6	65·5	81	76
	June	58·9	65·0	81·5	76
	July	58·8	65·5	80·5	75·5
	Aug.	59·9	66·5	80·5	75·5
	Sept.	61·4	66·5	81·5	75·5
	Oct.	60·8	65·5	81·5	75
	Nov.	60·8	65·0	81·5	74·5
	Dec.	60·8	64·0	81	74
1933	Jan.	60·3	62·0	80·5	72·5
	Feb.	59·5	61·0	79·5	71
	March	58·7	61·5	78·5	70·5
	April	58·5	61·5	77·5	70·5
	May	59·7	64·0	77·5	71
	June	61·2	66·0	79	71·5
	July	61·5	70·0	79·5	74
	Aug.	61·7	71·0	80·5	76
	Sept.	62·0	72·0	80·5	77
	Oct.	61·8	72·5	80·5	77
	Nov.	61·9	72·5	81·5	76·5
	Dec.	61·9	72·0	81	76

V

VALUATION OF STERLING

Purchasing Power Parities				
American Wholesale Prices ×4·86 / Board of Trade General	American Wholesale Prices ×4·40 / Board of Trade General	American Cost of Living × 4·86 / British Cost of Living	American Cost of Living × 4·40 / British Cost of Living	Monthly Average of Daily Rates
6·046	5·474	4·913	4·448	4·8550
5·968	5·403	4·943	4·475	4·8565
5·915	5·355	5·035	4·558	4·8585
5·808	5·258	4·947	4·479	4·8600
5·764	5·218	4·947	4·479	4·8641
5·754	5·210	4·889	4·426	4·8650
5·808	5·258	4·947	4·479	4·8566
5·963	5·399	4·918	4·453	4·8573
5·900	5·342	4·889	4·426	4·542
5·536	5·012	4·802	4·347	3·886
5·429	4·915	4·714	4·268	3·719
5·341	4·836	4·627	4·189	3·372
5·249	4·752	4·568	4·136	3·430
5·176	4·686	4·568	4·136	3·459
5·205	4·712	4·564	4·132	3·634
5·288	4·787	4·564	4·132	3·752
5·254	4·756	4·559	4·127	3·676
5·365	4·858	4·534	4·105	3·649
5·414	4·902	4·559	4·127	3·552
5·395	4·884	4·559	4·127	3·476
5·263	4·765	4·500	4·074	3·471
5·234	4·739	4·471	4·048	3·399
5·195	4·704	4·442	4·022	3·277
5·118	4·633	4·442	4·022	3·276
4·996	4·523	4·379	3·964	3·372
4·882	4·510	4·340	3·929	3·422
5·093	4·611	4·364	3·951	3·436
5·108	4·624	4·423	4·004	3·507
5·210	4·717	4·452	4·030	3·938
5·239	4·743	4·398	3·982	4·141
5·531	5·007	4·525	4·096	4·643
5·594	5·064	4·588	4·154	4·503
5·642	5·108	4·651	4·211	4·660
5·701	5·162	4·651	4·211	4·667
5·691	5·152	4·564	4·132	5·136
5·652	5·117	4·559	4·127	5·118

CHART No. 3

THE OVER-VALUATION AND UNDER-VALUATION IN STERLING IN TERMS OF THE U.S. DOLLAR, I.E. THE CO-EFFICIENT OF DEVIATION BETWEEN ACTUAL AND PURCHASING POWER PARITIES

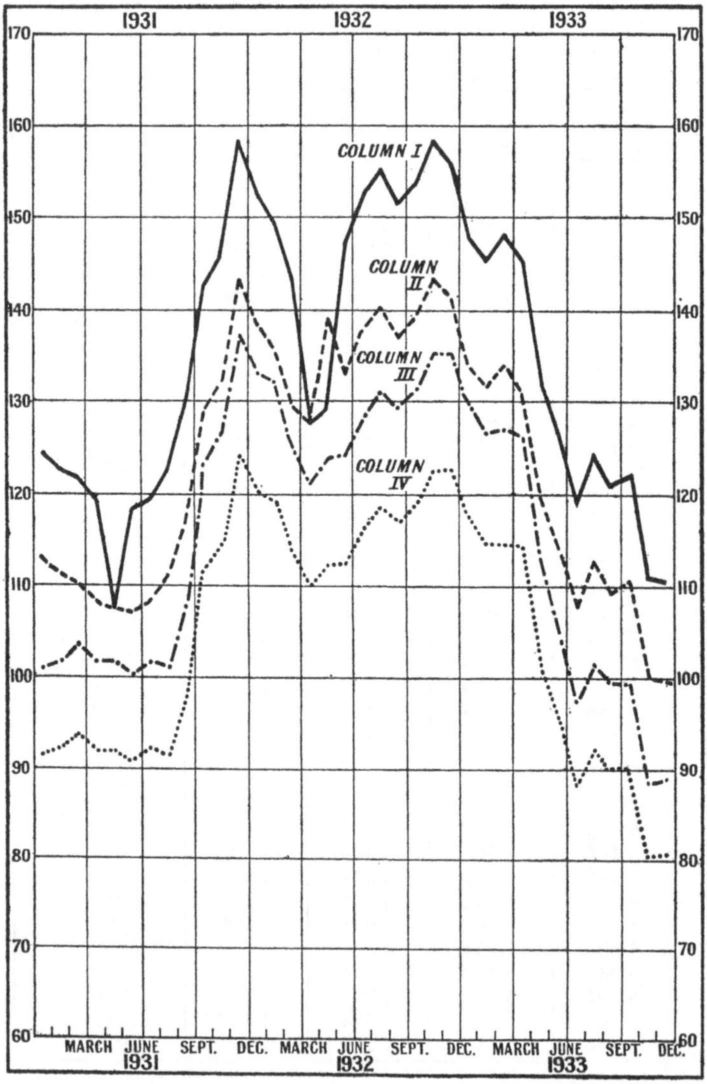

TABLE VI

CO-EFFICIENT OF DEVIATION BETWEEN ACTUAL AND PURCHASING POWER PARITY RATES

$$\text{i.e. } \frac{\text{P.P.Rate}}{\text{Actual Rate}} \times 100$$

Date.	Col. I American and British Wholesale Prices on Parity of \$4·86	Col. II American and British Wholesale Prices on Parity of \$4·40	Col. III American and British Cost of Living Prices on Parity of \$4·86	Col. IV American and British Cost of Living Prices on Parity of \$4.40
1931 Jan.	124·53	127·49	101·19	91·62
Feb.	122·87	111·25	101·78	92·14
Mar.	121·75	110·22	103·63	93·81
April	119·51	108·19	101·79	92·16
May	107·28	107·28	101·70	92·08
June	118·27	107·09	100·49	90·98
July	119·59	108·27	101·86	92·23
Aug.	122·76	111·15	101·25	91·68
Sept.	129·90	117·61	107·64	97·45
Oct.	142·46	127·98	123·57	111·86
Nov.	145·98	132·16	126·75	114·76
Dec.	158·39	143·42	137·22	124·23
1932 Jan.	153·03	138·54	133·18	120·58
Feb.	149·64	135·47	132·06	119·57
Mar.	143·23	129·66	125·59	113·70
April	127·58	127·59	121·64	110·13
May	129·38	139·39	124·02	112·27
June	147·03	133·13	124·25	112·50
July	152·42	138·01	128·35	116·19
Aug.	155·21	140·51	131·16	118·73
Sept.	151·63	137·28	129·65	117·37
Oct.	153·99	139·42	131·54	119·09
Nov.	158·53	143·54	135·55	122·73
Dec.	156·21	141·42	135·59	122·77
1933 Jan.	148·16	134·13	129·86	117·56
Feb.	145·59	131·79	126·83	114·82
Mar.	148·22	134·20	127·01	114·99
April	145·65	131·85	126·12	114·17
May	132·30	119·78	113·05	102·34
June	126·52	114·54	106·21	96·16
July	119·13	107·84	97·46	88·22
Aug.	124·23	112·46	101·89	92·25
Sept.	121·07	109·61	99·81	90·36
Oct.	122·16	110·61	99·66	90·23
Nov.	110·81	100·31	88·87	80·45
Dec.	110·43	99·98	89·08	80·64

Treasury is given power to borrow, and specifically, under Sec. 22 (6) of the Act of 1932, the 'Bank of England may advance to the Treasury any sums which the Treasury have under this section power to raise'. Three quite different sets of questions arise.

First, as to the technique of the operations.

1. So long as and whenever the Bank of England operates independently and is in a position to pay for the foreign funds which it buys by exchanging them for other assets in its books, the total volume of purchasing power placed at the disposal of the banking community is not affected. Technically, the foreign funds (dollars, francs) are placed in the Issue Department of the Bank and appear in the accounts under the rubric 'Other Securities'. If the Bank buys gold, it adds to the Gold Coin and Bullion in the same department. Since a purchase by the Bank adds to the amount of purchasing power available to the money market, the method by which such purchases can be prevented from swelling the net total of such funds is for the Bank to sell something to the market at the time when it is buying exchange. From the standpoint of the Bank such a simultaneous purchase and sale is, of course, equivalent to an exchange of this asset for another. Similarly, if the Bank disposes of some of its foreign assets or sells gold, this sale will only reduce total market funds if the Bank does not 'offset' the sale by the purchase of some other asset.

2. If the time comes when the Bank is not in a position to exchange one security for another in this way, and if its purchases of foreign exchange are not offset by sales of some other security, the purchases so made have the effect of swelling the total amount of market purchasing power; just as net sales without offsetting will reduce the total amount of market purchasing power. A net

increase in purchases must have the ultimate effect of raising the level of security values, of giving the money market the kind of funds which it regards as the equivalent of cash, of stimulating lending as soon as industrial and commercial conditions are favourable, and, therefore, of raising prices. Such a rise of prices would, of course, in itself help to bring any existing over-valuation to an end. If funds continue to be offered (or if the Bank continues to buy exchange and/or gold) a local boom may be stimulated, just as a continued influx of gold under normal gold standard conditions may stimulate a local boom. A net sale of assets will have, of course, precisely the opposite effects on the internal security and price level. Such a policy reduces undervaluation, if it exists, not by raising prices but by causing exchange to rise.

3. The Government, of course, possesses no free funds available for exchange operations. It must either borrow from the Bank of England or from the market. In so far as the Bank itself advances the purchase price, without selling other assets, the net effect will be the same as if it had bought the foreign exchange funds or the gold itself, i.e. in the long run a rise in the total volume of purchasing power will take place. In so far as the Bank lends effectively to the Government, but recoups itself by sales of other assets, or in so far as the Government refunds the Bank by borrowing in the open market, the addition to money market funds is for the time being offset by sales to the market or loans from the market. Once the Government Account has acquired a stock of gold and/or foreign exchange, sales of these funds will reduce indebtedness to the Bank (virtually, foreign holders of sterling funds or securities exchange them against gold or foreign exchange) or to the market. Sales, in so far as Government is indebted to the Bank, which

meanwhile has *not* offset its additional lending, reduce the volume of market funds; if the Bank has already offset and now offsets again, the net effect is to leave things unaltered. In so far as the Government borrowed directly from the market and now repays the loan, the effect is not to change the aggregate volume of funds at the disposal of the money market, but to change the direction in which they are used.

This brings one to the second of the questions involved, viz. the possible limits of action open to the Exchange Account. The direct effect of a purchase of gold or of foreign exchange by the Account is to weaken sterling when it is already falling, or to prevent a strengthening of sterling when it is already rising. So long as the Fund operates only with a fixed amount of money, it is powerless to prevent sterling falling when the whole of its resources have already been exhausted (i.e. when the assets consist entirely of gold and/or foreign exchange), unless it reverses its position and sells gold or exchange against sterling receipts. Similarly, when the pound is rising, the Account can only prevent a further rise by selling more sterling, which is the same thing as increasing the absolute size of the Account, if the whole of the amount has not already been invested. In fact, however, there is a method available for keeping the Fund affective, as an instrument of control, even without obtaining fresh Parliamentary sanction for an increase in the absolute amount of the Fund. Suppose the Fund invests its sterling reserves in gold or foreign exchange. It can sell this gold or foreign exchange to the Bank of England for cash. In this case, there will still be sterling available for further exchange operations. Even here there are limits. The Bank treats gold as if the sterling price of gold were still 84*s*. per fine ounce, whilst the market price is in the neighbourhood of 136*s*.

to 138*s*. sterling. Sales of gold must therefore weaken the Fund (by inducing losses) although they enable it to carry on operations upon a diminished scale. (These losses are, in one sense, purely nominal—since any *de jure* stabilization of the pound upon the basis of a lower gold content will be accompanied by a writing up of the sterling value of the gold stock of the Bank of England and the 'profit' arising from any such operations can be, or will be, used for the purpose of meeting any ultimate losses on the Exchange Equalization Account.) But what has been said will be sufficient to show that there are limits to the extent to which, once the Exchange Equalization Fund has started to invest its funds, it can continue to intervene. It would be a great misfortune if it were to be thought that a fund of this character could be a substitute for measures of a more radical nature which might prove to be necessary if the external or internal situation were again to alter violently in one direction or another.

The operations of the Exchange Equalization Account have been kept entirely secret: no official information has ever been vouchsafed as to the manner in which the assets of the Fund have been invested, the proportions of gold or foreign exchange held, the times at which changes in these assets have been made, or the principles by which the authorities are guided from time to time. Some light is thrown upon these matters by changes in the gold stock of the Bank of England[1] (though it is said that the Exchange Account also possesses gold of its own of unknown amount, nor does it follow that the gold acquisitions of the Bank have been entirely or even

[1] The gold stock of the Bank was on the average of 1931, 1932, and 1933, £140, £130, and £177 millions respectively. At the end of July 1934 it stood at £191½ millions, equal to £314 millions nominal if gold is taken at 138*s*. per fine ounce in place of the old mint price of 84*s*.

mainly due to the operations of the Account). But there have been episodes in recent international monetary history which throw indirect light upon what must have been the policy of those in charge of the Account. In the spring of 1932 the return flow of balances threatened to raise sterling, and the necessity of accumulating funds to repay the international loans made to this country before the final abandonment of gold must have led to purchases of foreign currencies upon a large scale: the flight from the dollar before the final crash in the U.S.A. and the flight from the franc must also have tended to raise sterling and the rise may have been kept down by purchases on official account: the foreign assets so acquired being turned into gold in order to reduce the risk of loss which might otherwise have occurred. The sharp decline in the dollar value of sterling in the autumn of 1932 (an accentuation of a normal seasonal movement) may also have been tempered by sales of dollars or other currencies and caused the Fund to consist more of sterling and less of other assets than it did before or has done since. The important point to remember is that, large as the absolute size of the Account is, 'normal' movements —including speculation and the shifting of the International Short Loan Fund from place to place—are also large, so that to regard the Fund as the ultimate determinant of exchange movements is in all probability a gross exaggeration.

CHAPTER V

THE CASE OF THE U.S.A.

OPINION AND policy in the sphere of monetary affairs have been so much influenced by the recent course of events in the United States and yet what has been happening there has been so little understood generally that an investigation of the American currency revolution is called for, especially as the future of the gold standard is closely bound up with the course of American policy.

In the case of Great Britain, certain clear-cut reasons can be given for the final catastrophe: in the final analysis they resolve themselves into the combination of international mistrust of Great Britain's position with the presence of certain definite maladjustments, viz. the inability, ever since the restoration of the gold standard in 1925, to adjust the level of costs to the extent demanded by Great Britain's peculiar dependence upon international trade coupled with the pursuance, in spite of this stumbling-block, of a policy of relatively free international lending. These factors could only be reconciled, in the absence of any other practicable alternative, by the process of 'borrowing short and lending long'. The position of the United States, it must be emphasized at the very beginning, was very different.

Firstly, the cost-structure in the United States was (and even after the recent legislation probably still is) much more elastic than that of Great Britain. In the mass-production industries costs were capable of drastic slashing in consequence of mechanical improvements: the absence of strong trade union organization meant that wages were less resistant to change (even if the decline in immigration worked in the opposite direction). The popularity of equity shares as instruments of stock market gambling and as investments meant that to a growing extent industries could reckon upon throwing on to the share-holding class the burden of depression by simply cutting dividends: the large extent to which industries financed themselves by re-investing profits in good years also worked in the direction of mitigating the inelasticity of the cost structure, in so far as that is represented by fixed interest charges. It is true that the American farmer was heavily indebted, but since agriculture is still largely a family unit of production, other elements in farm costs could be cut, even if mortgage and bank interest could not. Moreover, foreign trade is not of the same quantitative importance in the structure of American economic life as it is in that of Great Britain, even though certain branches of agriculture, e.g. cotton and tobacco growing, and certain industries, e.g. the motor-car and film industries, are greatly interested in foreign markets. The result of all these factors has been that at no time since the onset of the depression has public opinion been influenced by a fear that costs could not be adjusted to the international position of the country, nor has inelasticity of costs played a decisive role in the economic evolution of the last few years.

One must consider in the second place the position of the United States as a short and long term debtor of foreigners, for the vulnerability of the gold standard is in the first instance a function of the 'pull' which foreign creditors can exercise. The Department of Commerce issues annually the results of an investigation of the international banking position of the U.S.A. The figures for recent years are as follows[1] (million dollars):

[1] League of Nations, *Balances of Payments 1931 and 1932* (Geneva, 1933), p. 188.

	1929	1930	1931	1932
Total due to foreigners[1]	3,037	2,737	1,465	913
Total due from foreigners	1,617	1,802	1,239	1,058
Net liabilities or assets	−1,420	−935	−226	+145

It is, of course, true that of the American short-term assets abroad a certain proportion was 'frozen' in consequence of the German 'standstill agreements', exchange controls, and the illiquidity of foreign creditors. Making all possible allowance for these factors, it remains the case that America was ceasing to be a net debtor on short-term accounts, so that the danger to be apprehended on this ground was becoming more remote. In fact, the *external* 'flight from the dollar' had taken place earlier; the U.S.A. had sustained an international run both in 1931 and 1932, the outward and visible sign of this run being the sharp diminution of the gold stock in the autumn of 1931 and in the early summer of 1932. In spite of these manifestations, foreign confidence in the outlook in the U.S.A. was not undermined, a fact which is shown by the circumstance that in 1931 and 1932 alike there was a net *inflow* of long-term capital into the United States, which continued, though on a reduced scale, in 1933.[2] The gold stock of the country actually increased in 1932 by 53 million dollars, an outflow of 446 million dollars being more than offset by a net release from earmark of 458 million dollars. It is true that in the first three months of 1933 there was comparatively heavy earmarking of gold, viz., 370 million dollars, but

[1] i.e. Deposits, advances and overdrafts, short-term loans and investments, etc., and acceptance credits.

[2] *Vide* the Summary tables in *The Economist* of April 14th 1934. The excess of the purchase of dollar securities over new long-term loans by the U.S.A. was 218 million dollars, 217 million dollars, and 137 million dollars in 1931, 1932, and 1933 respectively.

these movements must be brought into relation with the country's gold stock, which at the lowest point in 1933 (end of March) still stood at 4,282 million dollars. So far as the danger of an *internal* drain is concerned, it must be remembered that in consequence of the passage of the Glass-Steagall Act on February 27th 1932 the Federal Reserve System had acquired the right to issue Federal Reserve notes backed by direct obligations of the Government of the United States. The desire to acquire current money, then, which was a characteristic feature of the American situation, could be satisfied without any direct pressure on the gold stock, for there is very little, if any, evidence that there was any heavy demand for gold, as distinct from currency, until the intensification of the crisis in the first three months of 1933—though there was, of course, a very considerable increase in the demand for hand-to-hand currency, which was in itself caused by, as well as causing, the banking crisis. A suspension of cash payments is no necessary consequence of a banking panic, though it was a feature of some of the previous crises through which the United States had passed. The Federal Reserve System was expressly created in 1913 for the purpose of avoiding any suspension of cash payments in the future, for the received tradition of central banking contains no place for a suspension of cash payments as a remedy for banking panic. On the contrary, the received tradition is that, so long as the foreign exchanges continue favourable, the way to avoid a suspension of cash payments is to lend freely against adequate security, but at a rate of interest sufficiently high to deter irresponsible borrowing and at the same time to attract back to the country a portion of its outstanding short-term assets. Even if it be held, as it quite plausibly may be, that under modern conditions a high bank rate does not attract funds, but on the contrary, accentuates the feeling of panic, there is nothing in the mere fact of banking pressure which warrants the abandonment of the gold standard, especially in view of the statistical and economic facts related above. The abandonment of gold in these conditions represents an arbitrary act of statesmanship, which may indeed be justified on political or psychological grounds, but which was certainly not inevitable on technical economic grounds.

It may perhaps be argued that, though the suspension of the gold standard (which was part of the series of measures which followed upon the crisis of March 4th when every bank in the country was closed) was not inevitable, regarded as one of the necessary instrumentalities for the restoration of confidence, it was impossible immediately to return to gold, suspension having once been decided upon; for the domestic and the foreign creditors of the banking system would have taken the precaution of acquiring gold, on the principle that a suspension having taken place once, there was no reason why it should not take place again if the situation did not improve in the immediate future. It cannot be denied that there is some force in this argument: on the other hand, it may with equal reason be argued that the suspension of the gold standard was calculated to give the impression, both at home and abroad, that the situation was even more serious than had been thought—with the consequence that the restoration of confidence was made more difficult than it would otherwise have been.

In fact, the abandonment of gold was not thought of in the initial stages as being permanent. Export licences seem to have been fairly easily obtainable and the level of the dollar in terms of gold currencies, though the dollar weakened, did not indicate any very pessimistic interpretation of the outlook. But the most striking and curious confirmation of that interpretation of the situation which is put forward here—that originally the abandonment of gold was regarded purely as a crisis phenomenon—is afforded by the circumstance that the abandonment of gold has come to be associated, not with the original proclamations of the President and the Emergency Legislation of March 1933, but with the issue of a further proclamation on April 20th 1933,[1] the terms of which are in fact intelligible only when studied in connexion with the preceding legislation. Technically the U.S.A. had abandoned the gold standard on March 4th: why, then, was such importance assigned to a proclamation issued nearly two months later? In my opinion, because it indicated a change in the point of view of the Administration, though it did not substantially alter the technical situation. In the course of these seven or eight weeks the policy of the country had undergone a change; though the abandonment of the gold standard was not really necessary as an element in crisis-policy, it was considered a necessary (even if only a negative) adjunct to the policy upon which the U.S. Administration was about to embark, viz., the policy of raising prices, if possible, back to the level of 1926.

American currency policy between April 1933 and the *de facto* stabilization of the dollar upon a gold basis in January 1934 falls into two sub-periods, only in the second of which did the deliberate depreciation of the dollar as an instrument of monetary depreciation play a decisive role, and then in a form which differentiates it

[1] The order of April 20th prohibited the earmarking and export of gold coin, bullion, and gold certificates, except when expressly permitted by Treasury licence in certain specified cases. For the technical reasons which have led me to the opinions expressed above, I refer to my article, 'Twelve Months of American Dollar Policy' in *Economica*, N.S., No. 2, pp. 122 et seq.

sharply from European experiments of a somewhat similar kind. In the first period, which extends from April to the end of October, one must distinguish between actual policy and the shaping of opinion which was to determine policy in the second period. The first period is marked by the following executive acts:

(1) The passage of legislation which permitted the President to implement, if he choose to do so, various inflationary measures. The so-called 'Inflation' or 'Thomas' Amendments to the Agricultural Adjustment Act,[1] which had been agreed to at a White House Conference by President Roosevelt as early as April 19th 1933 sanctioned the pursuit of a vigorous 'open-market' policy, allowed the issue up to a maximum of 3,000 million dollars of uncovered notes and, most important from our immediate standpoint, permitted the President to devaluate the dollar by proclamation, though the amount by which the gold content of the dollar was to be reduced was not to exceed 50 per cent. This was followed by the passage of the Joint Resolution of June 5th 1933 by which the 'Gold Clause' was abrogated, i.e. where contracts specified payment in United States gold coin of standard weight and fineness or specified payment in gold it was henceforward possible to satisfy the terms of the contract 'upon payment, dollar for dollar, in any coin or currency which at the time of payment is legal tender for public and private debts.'

(2) The rejection of the policy of immediate dollar stabilization. Such a policy would not have been inconsistent with the terms of the Inflation amendments just stated: it would have been possible to pursue an open market policy, or to issue greenbacks even if the gold content of the dollar had not been varied at all, and the amendments themselves specifically conferred the power

[1] This Act was approved May 12th 1933.

to give the dollar a determinate gold content again: all that the amendments *prevented* the President from doing in this respect was to reduce the gold content by more than a certain percentage. Moreover, the international situation was one which might have made dollar stabilization desirable, not only for its own sake, but as part of an internationally co-ordinated effort to restore sounder monetary conditions over a large part of the world. At the very moment when the so-called official abandonment of gold was being announced in Washington, the Prime Minister of Great Britain was upon his way across the Atlantic to confer with the President and a series of similar visits by other heads of European States was in prospect. These visits were in themselves undertaken in view of the forthcoming World Economic Conference, where monetary questions were bound to play a very considerable role. In the event the U.S. Government rejected the policy of stabilization with ever increasing emphasis: exchange stabilization was to be subordinated, first to the policy of raising prices and then to the policy of stabilizing prices at the higher level so attained. Having rejected on June 22nd the suggestion, emanating from the meeting of certain Treasury and Central Bank representatives, that exchange rates be *temporarily* stabilized during the London Conference, the President in a celebrated message on July 3rd also rejected the Joint Declaration, emanating from the Conference itself, which called for the *ultimate* restoration of the gold standard, the suppression of speculation in the foreign exchanges, and the maintenance of the *status quo* by the still existing gold standard countries. This declaration was rejected upon the ground that 'the sound internal economic system of a nation is a greater factor in its well-being than the price of its currency in changing terms of the currencies of other nations'. The object of American policy was to raise prices: 'the United States seeks the kind of dollar which a generation hence will have the same purchasing and debt-paying power as the dollar value we hope to attain in the near future'. This remained the official policy of the American Government throughout the period under review, and was re-emphasized in the broadcast message which inaugurated the second phase of policy, to which we shall come very shortly.

The policy of deferring stabilization until prices had risen, announced by the American Government, was on all fours with the attitude of the British Government on the problem, but, in the summer of 1933, there were pressing reasons for the refusal of the American Administration to commit itself. In the first place, there can be little doubt that in the spring of that year the depreciation of the dollar was one of the most potent factors in the rise of American security prices, and the American public has not yet learned to disregard the movement of security prices as an index of 'prosperity'. Moreover, under the combined influence of many factors, the fear of inflation, i.e. rising costs, and of the tendency of the new agricultural and industrial legislation to work in the same direction, a considerable boom was under way. It was natural to fear that if the dollar were stabilized these encouraging developments would come to an end. In fact, they were checked, but not by the stabilization of the dollar. There was a break in the stock and produce markets and a considerable fall in the volume of industrial production,[1] to which the relatively moderate improvement of the dollar in August may have contributed, an improvement which was in part perhaps influenced by the stabilization talk of previous months, but which was mainly due to other reasons.

[1] See table at foot of page 108.

Whatever the cause of the set-back, it represented a serious problem for the Administration. It had hitherto had no reason to press forward with the use of the Inflation amendments, but a check in the progress of recovery made it inevitable that public opinion would urge it forward to take more drastic action. In September, in fact, great pressure was being brought to bear upon the Administration, particularly by the agricultural States. To avoid worse things, perhaps, or merely because the President's advisers were convinced of the truth of the theory, the Government in October 1933 adopted a policy based upon the views of Professors G. F. Warren and F. A. Pearson of Cornell University: the agency most actively disseminating these views being a body of industrialists with headquarters in New York calling themselves the Committee for the Nation. The sum and substance of the point of view thus adopted can be stated in the words of the spiritual fathers of the policy themselves: 'A study of the history of prices shows that if the supply of the monetary unit is *suddenly*

	Industrial Production 1923–25 = 100	Exchange Rates. Am. Cents per 1 French franc.	Common Stocks 1926=100	Prices, 1926 = 100	
				All Commodities.	Farm Products.
Mar. 1933	56	3·936	43	60·2	42·8
Apl.	66	4·102	48	60·4	44·5
May	78	4·593	63	62·7	50·2
June	93	4·804	75	65·0	53·2
July	101	5·459	80	68·9	60·1
Aug.	91	5·375	75	69·5	57·6
Sept.	84	5·772	75	70·8	57·0
Oct.	76	5·817	70	71·1	55·7

(Data from *Federal Reserve Bulletin*)

doubled the price level doubles. Exactly the same results are obtained if the demand for the monetary metal is cut in half or if the amount of metal in the monetary unit is cut in half. Cutting the weight of metal in the monetary unit by half amounts to doubling the supply in so far as that country is concerned.'[1] Now if this proposition is rigidly true, the problem facing the United States could be easily and speedily solved: if the relation between the dollar and the 'monetary metal', i.e. gold, were varied in such a way as to raise the dollar value of gold, prices would rise in proportion to the fall in the gold value of the dollar, for every such fall in the gold value of the dollar would amount to increasing 'the supply in so far as that country [i.e. the U.S.A.] is concerned'.

Historically there is a connection between periods of rising gold production and of rising prices, and of falling gold production and falling prices. Further, if the total quantity of purchasing power is rigidly related to the output of the precious metal, and if no changes take place in the monetary habits of the population, i.e. 'velocity of circulation' is not affected, either by changes in quantity of money or other elements in the situation, this connection may be a fairly close one. But this proposition is a very different one from that advanced by Messrs. Warren and Pearson, for their argument stresses, not only the closeness of the connection, but the immediacy of the connection. Now, in fact, *time* is needed for two consequences of a change in the relation between the monetary metal and the money of a country to take effect: it takes time to adjust the quantity of purchasing power to the change in the gold content of the unit of account, and it takes time before a change

[1] Italics mine. From a Memorandum by Messrs. Warren and Pearson on the Business Situation, dated June 1st 1933.

in the quantity of money or purchasing power can influence prices. It does not follow that because, say, the content of the 'gold' dollar is halved and it is therefore possible on the basis of a given gold stock to double the amount of 'dollars' in circulation, the quantity of dollars in circulation will be immediately doubled. Still less does it follow that, if the quantity of dollars is doubled, all prices will be immediately doubled. In fact it is notorious that a considerable period of time is required before prices can adjust themselves, and even in a period of violent inflation some prices do not 'catch up' with the average. Indeed, it would never pay to inflate if prices did all adjust themselves at once. The attractiveness of inflation in a period of war, of revolution, or of depression, lies precisely in the differential effects it has upon the price level.

The policy actually announced at the end of October 1933 was justified to the country by President Roosevelt on the ground that the time had not yet come for a definite stabilization of the gold content of the dollar. To demand immediate exchange stabilization was to put the cart before the horse: 'to guess at a permanent gold valuation now would certainly require later changes caused by later facts'. On the other hand, in the President's opinion, the absence of *any* relation between the dollar and gold made the control of prices more difficult, since the dollar was 'altogether too greatly influenced by the accidents of international trade, by the internal policies of other nations and by political disturbances of other Continents. Therefore the United States must take firmly into its own hands the control of the gold value of our dollar. This is necessary in order to prevent dollar disturbances from swinging us away from our ultimate goal, namely, the continued recovery of our commodity prices.'

Between October 25th and October 29th the executive steps necessary to carry the policy into effect were announced: the Reconstruction Finance Corporation was empowered to buy gold at home and abroad and also to 'hold, earmark for foreign account, export, or otherwise dispose of such gold'.[1] The opening price was fixed at 31·36 dollars per fine ounce. For a time the policy of raising the gold price was vigorously pursued: it reached 33·56 dollars on November 14th and was 33·93 dollars at the end of that month. Then in the first fortnight of December it stood at 34·01 dollars: up to January 15th 1934 it stood at 34·06 dollars, and on January 16th was raised to 34·45 dollars. The old mint price of gold in the U.S.A. was 20·67 dollars: by the beginning of 1934, therefore, the increase in the dollar value of gold was 64·8 per cent. In the course of this phase of the American experiment the Government bought some 95 million dollars of gold, of which 21 million dollars approximately came from home production.

The experiment had two aspects: technical and economic. The technical aspect concerns the influence of the new gold-buying policy of the Government upon the international position of the dollar, i.e. its foreign exchange value. The new policy implied giving the dollar a determinate, if fluctuating, value in terms of gold. It follows from this that it gave the dollar a determinate even if fluctuating upper value in terms of gold currencies, e.g. the French franc. Thus, if an ounce of fine gold were saleable to the U.S. Government at

[1] Since the end of August the American Treasury had been buying newly-mined domestic gold at world prices, i.e. above the American mint price. This was done to satisfy the gold producers, who were, of course, hit by the fixed mint price. The new policy differed from this policy by the fact that (1) the Government, and not the market, fixed the new buying prices, (2) the gold bought at these prices was to be acquired at home *and abroad*: obviously two vital distinctions.

33 dollars per fine ounce, the United States dollar could not be worth more than the number of gold francs containing the same amount of gold, or purchasable for the same amount of gold. On the other hand, so long as the United States Government was not prepared to sell gold, then, though the dollar was not worth, and could not be worth, *more* than a maximum number of francs, it might be worth *less* than this number: for a fall in the franc value of the dollar (i.e. the number of francs a dollar could buy) would not necessarily result in an export of gold from the U.S.A. to France. But what, in these conditions, is the value of the dollar in terms of sterling?

It is a commonplace of the exchange market that all the various rates quoted in the market must move together in such a way that (given a free market) it is neither more nor less profitable to move funds from Centre A to Centre B directly than it is indirectly via Centre C, from which it follows that, if the rate between B and C alters, either the rate between A and C or A and B must also alter, or both rates must alter in opposite directions. If, then, the rate between New York and Paris altered, so that a given number of francs bought a larger number of dollars, that movement was bound to be accompanied by alterations, either in the New York-London rate, or the London-Paris rate, or in both rates together: since dollars became cheaper in Paris, they had to become cheaper in London, or the franc had to become dearer, or dollars became in part cheaper, whilst francs became in part dearer:[1] otherwise speculative operations would have been undertaken until the rates were 'in line' again. The dollar became, intrinsically, a cheaper

[1] A dearer franc would, of course, involve a higher London gold price. For the franc represents a certain weight of gold, and if the franc becomes dearer in terms of pounds, so must the amount of gold represented by a given number of francs.

coin. In consequence, if the value of the dollar in terms of pounds were not to alter, the value of the pound in terms of francs was bound to alter. If the value of the pound in terms of francs were not to change, the value of the dollar in terms of pounds was bound to change. It does not follow, however, that, because the external value of the dollar was thus made to fall, an immediate change in internal prices would result: the relation between the technical and the economic aspects is given by the possible divergence between percentage changes in the gold (or foreign exchange) value of the dollar and the alteration of the price-level inside the country. The dollar might become seriously undervalued, unless prices responded at once and uniformly to the change in the external value. Under the combined influence of the lowering of the gold value of the dollar and the pressure of speculative operations the dollar did fall heavily, attaining a low level of 5·50 dollars to the pound on November 22nd 1933 subsequently recovering to a maximum of 5·03 dollars. At the end of 1933 the dollar closed at 5·12 to the pound.

The direct influence of depreciation on prices comes, as we have already seen in the case of sterling, through import and export prices and through the reaction upon costs of production and cost of living. In the case of the U.S.A. the problem of determining the influence of currency depreciation is in any case made more difficult by the contemporaneous experiments in agricultural and industrial reorganization, which also tended to push the 'price level' or, at any rate, certain kinds of prices upwards. Since certain branches of American agriculture are more deeply influenced by the export situation than American industry in general, one would expect agricultural prices to be more influenced by the depreciation of the dollar than industrial prices, and this is perhaps

DOLLAR DEPRECIATION AND AMERICAN PRICES
(March 1933 = 100)

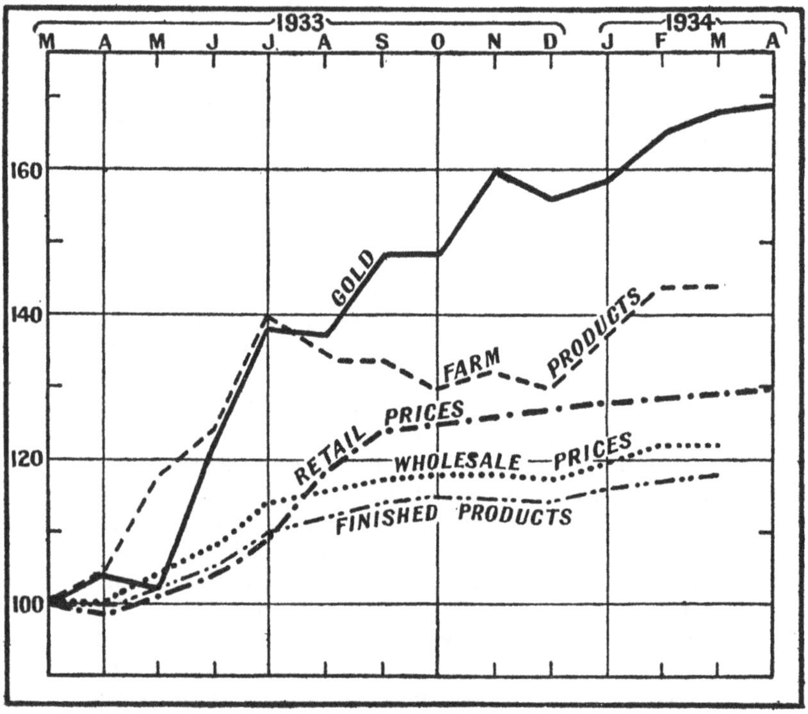

the case, though, to repeat, it is impossible to disentangle the influence of the N.R.A. and the A.A.A., and of other factors as well.

It is clear from the accompanying chart: (1) That of the various price-series quoted, that representing farm products moves most closely with the price of gold, but that the closeness of the movement is greatest in the early period, before, in fact, the policy of depreciating the value of the dollar by varying gold prices was ever adopted. (2) That in the second half of 1933 the movements in the gold price and in the price of farm products is rather divergent than congruent and that the two only begin to move together again after the close of the year, when the experiment was virtually at an end. (3) That retail prices, wholesale prices, and the prices of finished products show some rise, but it is quantitatively much less significant than the rise in the dollar value of gold and in the dollar value of farm products. These various movements, both in direction and scope, confirm *a priori* reasoning, but they also disprove the idea that a sudden alteration in the gold value of a currency must necessarily pull all prices in the desired direction. A little reflection will show that the form naturally adopted by the American experiment was hardly such as to give the Warren-Pearson theory full empirical verification. For the total volume of American purchasing power was not varied as the dollar-value of gold mounted; the total mass of purchasing power would only have increased if, every time the dollar value of gold rose, the gold stocks of the Central Bank had been re-valued and the increased purchasing power which could have been created on the basis of this re-valuation had been at once put into circulation. Even then, prices would in all probability have not responded at once; as it was, though the experiment in the autumn of 1933 was based upon the Warren-Pearson theory, the technical conditions under which its truth might have been experimentally confirmed or disproved were not really present.

In the early days of 1934, however, a new and decisive turn was given to American currency policy: the policy of depreciation was replaced by the policy of *de facto* stabilization. *De facto* stabilization did not appear as the first consideration of importance in the Presidential message in which Congress was invited to pass the appropriate legislation: the major preoccupation appeared to be the concentration of the entire gold stock of the country, including the vast holdings of the Federal Reserve System, in the hands of the Treasury of the United States. But the mobilization of gold required 'a more certain determination of the gold value of the American dollar'. Because of world uncertainties the President did not 'believe it desirable in the public interest that an exact value be now fixed'. Under the Agriculture Adjustment Act the President already possessed power to lower the gold content of the dollar by not more than 50 per cent: 'Careful study leads me to believe that any re-valuation at more than 60 per cent of the present statutory value would not be in the public interest. I therefore recommend to the Congress that it fix the upper limit of permissible re-valuation at 60 per cent.' Further, the President recommended the establishment of an Exchange Equalization Fund of 2,000 million dollars (£400 millions at par). By the Gold Reserve Act of 1934 these recommendations were carried out: this Act fundamentally altered the character of the American monetary system. The gold stock of the country became the property of the United States Government and the coinage of gold was to cease: the entire existing supply of gold currency was to be melted down into bars. The redemption of American currency was to cease except under Treasury regulations; substantially this means that America is now upon a gold bullion standard: the three main distinctions between the American system and the British system as it was between 1925 and 1931 consisting (1) in the presence of the Exchange Equalization Fund, (2) in the substitution of the Treasury for the Central Bank as the gold-buying agency, (3) in the absence of a definitive fixed gold value for the dollar—by the terms of the new legislation the weight of the dollar cannot be less than 50 per cent of the old weight of the dollar, but it cannot be more than 60 per cent. The actual *de facto* weight of the dollar was fixed by Proclamation on January 31st 1934 at $15\frac{5}{21}$ grains, $\frac{9}{10}$ fine, which is equal to 59·06 per cent of the former gold content of the gold dollar. Further, it was announced that, in accordance with the new determination of the weight of the dollar, the buying and selling price of gold would henceforward be 35 dollars per fine ounce. This price will of course last only as long as the President makes no use of the right to lower still further (i.e. to the 50 per cent limit) the gold content of the dollar: the Proclamation of January 31st expressly reserving the President's 'right by virtue of the authority vested in me to alter or modify the proclamation as the interest of the United States may require'. Up to the moment of writing (June 1934) no use has been made of the President's power to vary still further the gold content of the dollar.

A curious result has thus come about; for it will be remembered that it was primarily the attitude of the U.S.A. at the World Economic Conference which prevented the provisional stabilization proposed by the representatives of Treasuries and Central Banks and the acceptance of the Joint Declaration which, in however provisional a form, looked forward to the general re-establishment of the international gold standard.

The *de facto* stabilization of the dollar again raises the question of the technical and the economic consequences of the measure taken. Technically, the measure differed from the experiment previously tried by the fact that not only is there now a definite buying price for gold, but that there is also a definite selling price. It follows from this that, in terms of other gold currencies, the dollar can now not only not be worth more than a certain sum; it cannot now be worth less than a given sum of any other currency which is also upon gold. This involved an adjustment of rates of exchange to the new gold parities, which differed from those under the last gold price fixed under the gold-buying scheme (35·00 dollars per fine ounce against 34·45 dollars: thus each dollar represented a slightly smaller quantity of gold). The new parity with the gold franc, for instance, is 6·63 cents per franc. It was only gradually that the price of dollars in Paris fell to this point; at the end of January the price was still 6·26 to 6·28 American cents per French franc. The consequence was an immense outflow of gold to the U.S.A., for the amount of gold in a French franc, if exported and sold in the U.S.A., brought in 6·63 cents, whilst to buy dollars in Paris with the same amount of money brought in a smaller number of cents: to export gold was therefore very profitable and the very profitability of the operation meant that the number of dollars on sale in Paris would increase. This was so because the export of gold and its sale in New York meant that the exporters could sell dollars in Paris for francs, and this lowered the price of dollars, i.e., increased the number of cents which the franc could buy.[1]

[1] These changes in the franc-dollar relation had necessarily to affect also the relations between the London-Paris and London-

So far as the internal price level is concerned, the immediate effect of devaluation was, of course, nothing at all. But, owing to the fact that the total stock was re-valued, i.e., a larger number of paper dollars or of bank deposits could be built up upon the basis of the same physical weight of gold, the underlying position was capable of substantial change. The immense difference made to the *basis* of purchasing power as a consequence of re-valuation can be seen from the fact that 'the total stock of monetary gold in the United States increased from 4,033 million dollars on January 31st to 7,438 million at the end of February'.[1] The paper profit resulting from these operations has been credited to the United States Treasury at the Federal Reserve Banks. It has been drawn upon, both in consequence of the operations of the Exchange Equalization Fund and of the general expenditure of the United States Treasury, though so far it appears that the main direct effect has been that the banks, to whom cheques so drawn have been passed, have re-deposited them at the Federal Reserve Banks. The result is that the excess of the total reserve which they now hold over the reserves they are by law required to keep, i.e. the so-called 'Excess Reserves' of the Member Banks, are much larger than ever before in the history of the Federal Reserve System, notwithstanding seasonal increases in currency demand and repayment of loans to the Reserve System, both being factors which reduce the assets of the member banks with the Reserve Banks.[2]

New York rates and also the price of gold in London. Dollars were now cheaper in terms of francs, they had therefore to become cheaper in terms of pounds unless francs became dearer in terms of pounds, in which case the price of gold in London would rise. If dollars became *dearer* in terms of pounds, francs would have to become dearer still and the price of gold in London would rise still more.

[1] *Federal Reserve Bulletin*, March 1934, p. 141.

[2] Ibid, p. 142.

The possibility of a considerable expansion in the volume of loans is therefore present, and if the U.S.A. Government were to make use of the power it already possesses to devaluate the dollar by a further 10 per cent of its original gold content, the excess reserves and, with them, the potential expansion of bank loans, would rise still more. In the period immediately following the devaluation of the Austrian, German, and French currencies, a direct stimulus to credit expansion was afforded by the under-valuation of the currencies at the parity rate chosen, combined with the influx of capital upon a large scale and there came what I have elsewhere called the 'Stabilization Boom'.[1] It is unlikely that similar consequences will follow *directly* from the United States stabilization, but the vast expenditure of the United States Government, coupled with a return of confidence, or followed by such a return, whether or not expenditure on the present scale is maintained, would work in the same direction. Whatever initiated the expansion in the demand for bank loans, it would not be easy for the Reserve System to check it without sacrificing a larger proportion of its remaining earning assets than might be technically possible to effect without breaking the market in Government securities and imperilling its own income, though this latter consideration is a minor one. At the end of April 1934, for instance, the total earning assets of the Federal Reserve Banks amounted to 2,440 million dollars, of which amount all but 9 millions consisted of United States Government securities. 460 million dollars of these were held against Federal Reserve Notes and Federal Reserve Bank Notes. Excess reserves stood in the neighbourhood of 1,700 million dollars and total member reserves at 3,750 million dollars. Thus the

[1] Cf. my *First Year of the Gold Standard*, especially pp. 20 et seq.

total earning assets available for sale, approximately 2,000 million dollars, were only 300 million dollars more than the excess reserves. It would appear, then, that the possibility of a dramatic rise of prices is not excluded: the only practicable alternative would be to utilize the powers already conferred on the Reserve System by a section of the Agricultural Adjustment Act, 1933, which has received little notice (Sec. 46), by which the Federal Reserve Board 'upon the affirmative vote of not less than five of its members and with the approval of the President, may declare that an emergency exists by reason of credit expansion, and may by regulation during such emergency increase or decrease from time to time in its discretion the reserve balances required to be maintained against either demand or time deposits'. The use of these emergency powers to increase the minimum reserve requirements of the member banks would of course reduce, not the total reserves of the member banks, but their *excess* reserves, would make 'open market' operations tell more quickly, and, by forcing the banks to support additional loans by direct borrowing from the Reserve System, would restore to some extent the power of the System to control the rate of expansion.

CHAPTER VI

THE GOLD STANDARD IN RECENT OFFICIAL LITERATURE

IT MUST not be imagined that so far-reaching a catastrophe as the destruction of the international standard of value, which had been restored at such great cost during the decade between the end of the War and the collapse of the boom in 1929, has been neglected by the governments of the world. On the contrary there has been in the last five years an almost continuous international discussion of the problem of the standard: an interchange of view which culminated in the unfortunate World Economic Conference of 1933 and which may be said to have begun with the appointment of the Gold Delegation of the Financial Committee of the League of Nations in 1929 (that is, before the crisis had become really acute) for the purpose of examining into and reporting upon 'the causes of fluctuations in the purchasing power of gold and their effect upon the economic life of the nations'.[1] The special circumstances of Great Britain led to the appointment in the late autumn of 1929 of the Committee on Finance and Industry, charged to inquire into banking, finance and credit, 'paying regard to the factors, both internal and international, which govern their operation'.[2] These agencies which had been created to deal with problems which arose before the almost universal abandonment of gold found themselves obliged to face new problems of hitherto unsuspected

[1] Apart from special items of memoranda, etc., submitted to it, the Gold Delegation has published the following: *First and Second Interim Reports* (September 1930 and January 1931) and a *Final Report* issued in June 1932 (C. 502, M. 243, 1932 II A).

[2] Reported as Cmd. 3897 of 1931.

magnitude as time went on. The Lausanne Conference, called upon to liquidate the problem of Reparations, ended by inviting the League to call a conference for deciding upon the 'measures to solve the other economic and financial difficulties which are responsible for and may prolong the present world crisis'. The Lausanne Conference was followed by the meeting of the representatives of the British Empire at Ottawa, and the Ottawa Conference also dealt with the problems of money and the international standard from the standpoint of the constituent members of the Commonwealth. In the early part of 1933 there appeared the 'Draft Annotated Agenda'[1] submitted to the League by the Preparatory Commission of Experts, which was in due course followed by the record of the decisions at the World Economic Conference[2] itself. The events at that Conference were responsible for important statements of principle by the members of the British Empire and of the 'Gold Bloc', i.e. those European countries still upon the gold standard. Finally, there exists—apart altogether from the appropriate committees of the League of Nations—a new centre for the continuous study and discussion of international monetary questions: the Bank for International Settlements, itself a child of the Young Conference on reparations. The present state of international opinion finds its appropriate medium of expression in the last available annual report of the Bank—the 'Bankers Club' as it is sometimes called.[3] The volume of official literature is thus very considerable: in order to view the future of the gold standard intelligibly, it is necessary to understand

[1] Reported as Cmd. 4174 and 4175 of 1932.

[2] Official No. C. 48 (1), M. 18 (1) 1933 II and C. 435, M. 220 1933 II, *Reports approved by the Conference on July 27 1933 and resolutions adopted by the Bureau and the Executive Committee.*

[3] *Bank for International Settlements: Fourth Annual Report.* Basle: May 1934.

the course of recent official discussion. The fact that this discussion has hitherto not led to any positive result is apt to mislead: whilst it would be futile to pretend that there is unanimity upon the ultimate objectives of the gold standard, it still remains true that there is much more agreement upon this point than there is upon the question immediately facing the world, viz. the conditions upon which it would be desirable to return to the gold standard. This, the major question of tactics, is the real bone of contention. It does not follow, of course, because a greater measure of agreement has been obtained with regard to the way in which the gold standard should be manipulated, once it has been restored, than over the conditions under which the gold standard should be restored, that there is nothing left to be said upon the former point. It might well be the case that the trend of official opinion has lagged somewhat behind and that professional economic opinion is no longer so whole-heartedly in favour of the course of action which commends itself to official opinion as it was at one time. This particular issue, however, can well be left over to the next chapter: what concerns us at the moment is the actual course of official thought.

I. *The ultimate objective: the restoration of the gold standard.* There is a general consensus of opinion that the ultimate objective of monetary policy must be the restoration of the gold standard. Upon this particular point there is no difference of opinion between the so-called 'Expert' Committees and the Diplomatic Conferences, nor between the members of the Sterling Group and the members of the Gold Bloc. The 'ultimate aim of monetary policy', the Ottawa Resolutions urge, 'should be the restoration of a satisfactory *international* monetary standard', a point of view reiterated in the Joint Declaration of the members of the British Commonwealth after the failure of the World Economic Conference: 'The undersigned delegations now reaffirm their view that the ultimate aim of monetary policy should be the restoration of a satisfactory international gold standard. . . .' The Final Report of the Gold Delegation emphasized the belief of the Delegation 'that, at the present stage of world economic development, the gold standard remains the best available monetary mechanism'. The Preparatory Commission of Experts in their Draft Annotated Agenda for the World Economic Conference urged that among the four principal questions which the Governments would have to consider, 'in the field of monetary and credit policy, the objective must be the restoration of an effective international monetary standard to which those countries which have abandoned the gold standard can wisely adhere'. First among the resolutions unanimously adopted by a Sub-Commission of the Monetary and Financial Commission of the World Economic Conference was the following: 'That it is in the interests of all concerned that stability in the international monetary field be attained as quickly as practicable: that gold should be re-established as the international measure of exchange values, time and parity being for each country to determine.' But this practical unanimity of view as to the ultimate objective does not prevent a profound difference of view as to the methods by which it is to be attained.

II. *The major question of tactics: immediate stabilization or price-lifting as the next step.* Almost as soon as Great Britain had abandoned the gold standard there developed in official circles—perhaps it is better to say in governmental circles, since the attitude of the Bank of England is less clear upon the point—the view that before Great Britain could safely return to the gold standard the level of prices, both in terms of gold and in terms of sterling, must rise. This fundamental condition —not by any means the *only* condition, be it noted—has governed British policy since that time, and has been stated time after time by the Chancellor of the Exchequer, and has been adopted by the British Commonwealth Group. The Ottawa Conference Resolution, for instance, made it a condition precedent to the restoration of gold that there should be a 'rise in the general level of commodity prices in the various countries to a height more in keeping with the level of costs, including the burden of debt and other fixed and semi-fixed charges'. The dissentient members of the Gold Delegation, in their separate report, also urge that the 'most effective measure that could be taken at the present moment in order to pave the way for a restoration of the gold standard as an international monetary system would be to raise the general price level in the gold standard countries.' Again, in his speech at the Fourth Plenary Meeting of the World Economic Conference, the Chancellor of the Exchequer, sketching 'in broad outline the policy of the U.K. Government on the questions before the Conference' repeated the view that 'Firstly it was essential to bring about a recovery in the world level of wholesale commodity prices sufficient to yield an economic return to producers of primary commodities and to restore equilibrium between costs and prices . . . generally.' The first paragraph of the draft resolution submitted to the Monetary and Financial Commission by the British Delegation on June 20th also expressed the same point of view.[1] The view that concerted or individual efforts to raise prices should take precedence over immediate attempts to stabilize exchange was shared by the U.S. Government and, as already set

[1] *Vide Journal of the Monetary and Economic Conference*, No. 10, p. 70.

forth, formed the keynote of President Roosevelt's message of July 3rd to the Conference, a message which effectively put an end to the effort to arrive at a parity at which provisional stabilization could be agreed upon by the countries primarily interested.

To refuse to consider a return to gold without a previous rise of prices having taken place of course leaves open the whole question as to the best method of raising prices. It is also perfectly consistent with the view that other factors, besides monetary, have been responsible for the depression and with the view that other conditions, as well as a rise in the price level, must be satisfied before a return to gold can be safely undertaken. The British view, in fact, as officially presented, has never been so clear-cut as to exclude all considerations other than a rise in the price-level: neither the Macmillan Report[1] nor the official utterances of the Government since that time have failed to insist upon the very complicated nature of the problem to be solved. Nor was the attitude of the gold standard countries as unsophisticated as is sometimes imagined. There is not the slightest inconsistency between desiring a prior return to the gold standard and desiring to see a rise in the price level: for it may perfectly legitimately be argued that without

[1] *Macmillan Report*, paragraph 277. 'We have concluded that a restoration of the international price level should be a prime object of international statesmanship. How far such a restoration of the international price level is in fact feasible is, however, a further question. We believe that the outcome is likely to depend in part on a complex conjunction of economic factors in the world at large of a kind which is not directly controllable at the centre.' Cf. The Chancellor of the Exchequer at the World Economic Conference (second meeting of the first Sub-Commission of the Monetary and Financial Commission when introducing the British resolution): 'But these measures, though essential, were not sufficient. There must also be restoration of the confidence which had been destroyed through adverse economic and political conditions.' (*Journal* No. 10, p. 70, col. 2.)

firm ground under one's feet, in the shape of an international standard, confidence cannot be restored and, without a return of confidence, recovery, in the shape of a rise of prices, is impossible. The truth is that at the World Economic Conference the representatives of the Gold Bloc countries by no means took a unanimous view as to the importance of a rise of prices *per se*: the only outspoken sceptic on this point was the representative of Italy.[1] What the representatives of the Gold Bloc insisted upon was that the continuance of a state of chaos in the monetary field was intrinsically undesirable and was likely to worsen rather than improve the situation: but this left the question of the desirability of a rise of price open.

Once it is admitted that 'confidence' plays a role in the formation of the price level, the clear-cut line of opposition between the 'stabilizers' and the 'price-raisers' becomes more blurred than appears at first sight. From the technical point of view, the choice does not lie between an immediate return to the gold standard and the retention of a purely 'free' paper currency: it is perfectly possible to agree to a *de facto* stabilization without a final and irrevocable decision as to the ultimate parity to be chosen. This very important point will require further consideration in the final chapter of this book: at this stage it is only necessary to draw attention to the existing differences of standpoint as regards the question of the immediate procedure to be followed.

III. *The technique of Price Raising*. Supposing it to

[1] *Journal of the Monetary and Economic Conference*, No. 4, p. 13, col. 1, 'A rise in the monetary expression, for example, of prices could not stimulate economic recovery. Present problems would reappear intensified as soon as an inversion in the present downward price tendency set in. . . . The present hardships . . . had their roots outside the monetary field and monetary manœuvres would not remove them but would make them worse in the end.'

be agreed that some rise of prices is desirable, then the question of how this rise is to be brought about is of paramount importance. Now a rise of prices can be brought about by monetary means only if the efforts of the monetary authorities are not countered by action on the part of the money-using population. An unbalanced budget does result in direct expenditure by Government, but the psychological effects may be disastrous, in so far as they result in the business world anticipating further trouble in the future, so that increased expenditure on the part of Government leads to an unwillingness to adventure on the part of others. Similarly, the threat to lower the value of money in the future, i.e., the inculcation of a fear of future 'inflation' (primarily through the financing of an unbalanced budget or of public works or of unemployment relief through Central Bank advances rather than through borrowing in the open market) may stimulate business for the time being by inducing a flight from the currency into commodities or equity shares. On the other hand, if the apprehensions are universally entertained, the only effect of playing upon the fear of inflation may be, as was urged by a French delegate to the World Economic Conference, that hoarding of goods may be substituted for the hoarding of money. A policy of public works has the effect of causing an immediate increase in the volume of employment in the 'public works industries' and in the ancillary industries dependent thereupon: on the other hand it may cause a decline in the volume of constructional work which would otherwise have been carried out by private persons and corporations. Public works financed by borrowing keep up the rate of interest and the psychological effects may be deterrent in other ways—as, for instance, by inducing a belief that the situation is bad 'otherwise the Government would not have tried these expedients,' etc. If the public works are financed by inflation pure and simple, the psychological effect may be the same as with inflation for the sake of balancing the budget. To all this has to be added the fact that more normal methods of stimulating recovery, i.e. by large scale purchase of securities by the Central Banks for the purpose of raising bond prices and therefore lowering the effective rate of interest upon first-class bonds (thus encouraging new issues and new investment), may simply result in the accumulation of large masses of reserve cash or 'excess reserves' which cannot be employed except at very low rates of interest in the short-term money market. 'Cheap money' may bring about the desired results in the long run, but there is a general agreement among economists that the 'run' may be longer than optimists sometimes imagine. In this respect a remarkable change of standpoint has come over the economic world in recent years. It was possible for the Macmillan Committee to argue that 'no one would doubt the ability of a closed monetary system to bring about a rise of prices: *in fact it is only too easy*'.[1] I am inclined to think that to-day the view—always held by certain economists of note, e.g. Mr. R. G. Hawtrey—that the power of Central Banks to raise prices *in a depression* was subject to definite limitations is more widely appreciated than it was even a relatively short time ago.

It becomes necessary to ask, then, how the technical problem of raising prices is envisaged in recent official reports and documents. In general, the line is conservative, in the sense that reliance is placed primarily upon the effects of 'cheap money', uninfluenced by the deterrent effects which might be produced by unbalanced

[1] *Report*, p. 118. Cf. *Final Report of Gold Delegation*, Minority Report, p. 68.

budgets or public works. The Ottawa Conference urged a policy of low rates of interest and an abundance of short-term money; 'favourable monetary conditions should be achieved, not by the inflationary creation of additional means of payment to finance public expenditure, but by an orderly monetary policy, safeguarded, if the necessity should arise, by such steps as will restrain and circumscribe the scope of violent speculative movements in commodities or securities'. The Annotated Agenda submitted by the Preparatory Commission of Experts calls upon countries with a free gold standard to practise an open-market policy designed to provide a plentiful supply of credit: 'to pursue a liberal credit policy, characterized by low money rates in the short-term market and a reduction of long-term money rates by conversions and other operations as far as feasible' whilst on balance rejecting the policy of public works: if such a policy, they say, 'were not kept within reasonable limits, and if it were to result in deteriorating Government credit, debt conversions might be interfered with and the lowering of long-term interest rates delayed'. They look to recovery coming as the result of a revival of confidence, itself generated as a result of 'political and monetary authorities endeavouring to carry out a policy which holds out some hope of ultimate improvement'.

It does not follow that because so much emphasis is placed in these documents upon 'cheap money' as a solution that ancillary methods of recovery are not stressed: that is not so. There is a general recognition of the fact that the depression has been deepened and the fall of prices has been made worse by the cessation of international lending and the intensification of economic nationalism: the first is a natural result of the unwillingness of the investor to lend to those raw material producing areas which, because their products have fallen most heavily in price—a fall itself in large measure due to forced sales in consequence of the cessation of loans: the second is a consequence of the depression and particularly of the under-valuation of currencies. Such under-valuation destroys the efficacy of protection and leads naturally to the adoption of special quota and licensing devices designed to prevent the fall in the value of paper currencies from stimulating exports. There is a growing recognition in official international literature that stabilization, the resumption of lending, and the inauguration of a regime of freer trade all hang together. The future of international lending and the tariff question have a wider significance: the working of the gold standard, if and when restored, is intimately associated with these questions. They constitute, not only short-term issues, but vital aspects of the long-term problem as well.

IV. *Technical aspects of the gold standard.* If there is still considerable opposition of views as to what ought to be done immediately, the course of international discussion has made much clearer the conditions under which, and under which alone, the gold standard can function successfully. Certain positive and negative conditions must be fulfilled: their nature is set out below.

(*a*) The fundamental assumption of the gold standard is that it should be an international system, and must be worked in the light of a general understandng of what an international system implies. 'It is impossible', remarks the Preparatory Commission of Experts, 'to maintain an international monetary system except on the basis of an international economic system', and it is impossible to maintain an international economic system except upon the twofold condition that the economic life of particular areas is capable of adjusting itself to changes coming from without, whilst at the same time the collectivity of states forming the system must be prepared to face the consequences in the outside world resulting from large-scale changes in an important member of the collectivity.[1] It goes without saying that this mutual adjustment of the part to the whole, and the whole to the part, is a matter of the greatest delicacy in practice; since it involves, not only the right of 'self-determination' on the part of the various monetary authorities, but also the exercise of practical judgment. There is also growing recognition of the fact that some disturbances of international equilibrium, induced by changes within an important country or group of countries, may be of a character not calling for international action, or for offsetting action within the part affected, whilst others are of such a character. It is this necessity for international equilibrium, on the one hand, and the difficulty of deciding the true character of disturbing factors, on the other, which are responsible for the emphasis now universally placed upon the technique of co-operative action.

(*b*) International co-operation and the framing of the rules of the 'gold standard game'. These matters cannot be separated: co-operation involves a basis of mutual understanding, and mutual understanding, given the technical nature of the subject-matter, involves, if not common action, at least action which is not self-contradictory, i.e. which must be co-operative in the sense that it is directed to a common end. The need for co-operation in a complicated world is indeed self-evident, and has been stressed by all the reporting authorities, from the Macmillan Committee onwards.[2]

[1] Cf. with this the significant assertion of paragraph 19 of the *Final Report of the Gold Delegation* (*Report*, p. 12).

[2] *Report*, paragraphs 240–1 and elsewhere: *Gold Delegation, Final Report*, paragraph 206 and paragraph 232: *Annotated Draft*

The difficulty has lain, not in any absence of a desire to co-operate, but in the absence at times of common principles of action: moreover, as already pointed out, the degree of international co-operation in the recent past has been greater than the critics sometimes suppose.[1]

(c) *Gold Economy and Reserve Ratios*. Before the onset of the depression the possibility of gold shortage with its effects upon the long-period price level was much canvassed among technical experts and was indeed one of the reasons for the appointment of the Gold Delegation of the League. The fall in prices and the consequential stimulus to gold production have for the moment at least made the problem of gold shortage—viewed as a long-period issue—seem somewhat remote: the imminent gold shortage previously feared is farther off than ever. Nevertheless, the discussion of the prospective gold shortage has left a permanent mark upon the literature of the gold standard: it has led to a realization of the desirability of reducing the lock-up of gold supplies involved in the maintenance of existing reserve ratios. Post-war legislation upon the subject of gold reserves tended on the whole to tighten up the regulations, thus tending to undo the economizing effects of the disappearance of gold from actual circulation as coin, since, in order to comply with the regulations, it was necessary to hold a 'free reserve' of gold over and above the statutory minimum, and this itself tended to raise the absolute demand for gold. It is now universally agreed that minimum reserve requirements should be reduced, if not abandoned altogether: and the argument is reinforced by an appeal to the circumstance that one method of enforcing gold economy, viz. the widespread use of the gold exchange standard, is likely to be less popular in

Agenda, p. 17, S.I.3 (c): Resolution 3 of the *Monetary Commission of the World Economic Conference*.

[1] See above, p. 34.

the immediate future owing to the losses sustained by certain Central Banks when the countries in which they had been in the habit of keeping part or the whole of their reserves themselves abandoned gold.[1]

(*d*) *International debts, international lending and the tariff problem.* It was noticed above (Section III) that the possibility of restoring the gold standard without a resumption of international lending and some mitigation of the severities of the existing tariff regime has been seriously questioned: that the working of the gold standard as a permanent institution of the economic world is bound to be influenced by the loan and tariff policy pursued was made clear in Chapter I (p. 15 et seq). The malignant influence exerted by the effort to settle non-commercial indebtedness at a time of falling prices and increasing tariff barriers is a point of agreement between the various schools of thought whose views diverge sharply on some of the matters discussed in previous sections. Thus the signatories of the Minority Report of the Gold Delegation attributed the *direct* responsibility for the depression which began in 1929 to the effort to continue inter-governmental payments, at a time when the willingness of the United States and France to lend abroad in such a way as to offset the effect, which debt payments would otherwise have had, had ceased.[2] Though a discussion of inter-governmental debts

[1] Resolution I (d) of the Monetary Commission of the World Economic Conference recommended that 'in so far as the system of percentage gold cover is applied a minimum ratio of not more than 25 per cent should be considered as sufficient; similar elasticity should be achieved by appropriate measures where other systems are applied. However, such changes must not be taken as an excuse for unduly building up a larger superstructure of notes and credits: in other words, the effect of this resolution should be to increase the free reserve of Central Banks and thereby to strengthen their position.'

[2] *Final Report*, p. 66, and cf. Professor Cassel's *Memorandum of Dissent*, p. 75.

was excluded from the deliberations of the World Economic Conference, a settlement of inter-governmental debts was expressly alluded to by the Preparatory Committee in their Annotated Agenda as 'of particular value' in arriving at the solution of the problem of rebuilding the gold reserves of certain countries. The absolute necessity of dealing satisfactorily with the problem of tariffs, quotas, exchange restrictions, etc., has also been emphasized in all the documents under review: there is a general insistence upon the desirability of securing that debtors shall be allowed to liquidate their debts in goods and services: otherwise exaggerated gold movements are inevitable.

(*e*) There remain for mention two monetary problems, the bearing of which upon the functioning of the gold standard is indeed sufficiently obvious. The first of these is the constant menace presented to the smooth working of the gold standard by the existence of a great mass of international balances. Great Britain was driven off gold because of a 'flight from sterling' by the holders of such balances, and it is clear that, in so far as the world must reckon with a permanent increase in the volume of such balances, a new element of instability is present, to which pre-war experience affords no parallel. At the present time over a part of the area nominally adhering to the gold standard these balances are 'frozen' and are subject to an elaborate network of regulations of various kinds.

The Second Interim Report of the Gold Delegation made some suggestive remarks relating to this problem. The first was that the problem of the 'invisible items' was made much more difficult by commercial policies which impeded the free movements of goods and services: 'What is necessary for the normal working of the gold standard is that there should be a smooth flow from country to country alike of goods, services, and securities. Only then can short-term capital perform its proper function of allowing temporary accommodation in such a way as to lesson and not occasion gold transfers.' The second suggestion was to the effect that 'the sensitiveness of liquid capital has been due not so much to its magnitude' as to 'unstable economic and political conditions'. If this is accepted as a reasonable explanation, as indeed it must be, it links the question of currency reform up with very wide issues indeed. The Preparatory Commission dealt with the problem, not from the long-run angle, but from the short-run point of view, i.e. in its connection with standstill agreements, exchange restrictions, and transfer moratoria. The existing system was condemned as placing 'good and bad debtors on a footing of equality' and the Commission demanded its replacement 'by a definite solution which would take into account the circumstances of each individual case'. But this obviously leaves the long-run problem where it was: so far as the permanent working of the gold standard is concerned, here is a new problem of great significance.

A word must finally be said as to the treatment accorded to the problem of the Gold Exchange Standard in recent literature. The Second Interim Report of the Gold Delegation drew attention to the fact that the Gold Exchange Standard 'has somewhat complicated the mechanism of the international system by distorting in certain cases the reciprocal effect of the transference of central banking reserves. . . . An export of gold from one country to another used to set in motion reverse sequences of events in the exporting and in the importing countries. If the reserve consists of foreign assets, however, such reciprocal changes need not necessarily take place at the same time. The exact effect of a transfer of the claims which such assets represent will depend on how these assets are held and betweeen what countries the transfer takes place.'[1] The Preparatory Commission, whilst agreeing that the gold exchange standard had in practice revealed 'some grave defects', nevertheless though the adoption of the system 'may for many countries hasten their return to an international standard and will form an essential feature in the permanent financial arrangements of the countries which have no highly developed capital markets'. Some of the dangers of the system could be avoided if such foreign exchange reserves were invested through or with 'the Central Bank of the currency concerned or with the Bank for International Settlements. This is all the more important because it is . . . imperative that Central Banks should have a complete knowledge of all the operations of the Central Banks on their markets . . . it is important that each Central Bank which employs foreign exchange balances should take all necessary measures in order to secure itself against the risk of foreign investments.'[2]

V. *The Ultimate Objectives of the Gold Standard.* Just as it is impossible to dissociate the question of international co-operation between monetary authorities and the basis of co-operation on the other, so it is impossible to discuss what have become known as the 'rules of the gold standard game' from the ultimate objectives which it is hoped to attain through the instrumentality of that standard. The practical difficulties arise from the fact that the attainment of a long-period objective, be it the stabilization of the general level of wholesale prices, or any other, must take account of the circumstance that

[1] *Report*, p. 13.

[2] *Draft Annotated Agenda*, p. 16. See also the discussion in *Final Report of the Gold Delegation*, paragraphs 215–21, which, however, deals mainly with other aspects of the problem of the gold exchange standard than those relevant here.

short-period elements of great importance necessarily enter into the day-to-day working of the gold standard from the standpoint of the constituent members of an international gold standard system. The gold standard is not only a means of attaining certain long period objectives, such as, for instance, the maintenance of a certain level of prices; it is also a method of conserving international equilibrium: or, as I have previously termed it, of keeping the price and income structures of particular countries in touch with one another. The traditional task of the Central Banks and other monetary authorities has been to conserve international equilibrium: for it is only in the post-war decade that other objectives have come consciously to the forefront at all. The old objectives remain: the main scientific problem of the gold standard to-day is to test the congruence of various objectives, new and old, and to devise an appropriate technique.

Discussion of the long-period objective turns round the concept of stabilization: and it is significant that the course of international discussion should have gradually revealed the unsatisfactory character of any simple form of definition of what is wanted. The earlier discussion rested upon the view that what was wanted was the attainment of, and the adherence to, a given price level statistically defined; though even the earlier definitions allow a glimpse of the true difficulty to be seen. Thus the Macmillan Report laid it down that the 'main objective of Central Banks' acting in co-operation was to 'maintain the stability of international prices both over long periods and over short periods—i.e. they should both keep the average steady over a period of years and avoid fluctuations round this average from year to year. *Or alternatively—if this alternative were to receive inferior support—they should prevent prices from falling to a greater extent than is justified by the increase in the efficiency of production.*'[1]

These italicized words already show that 'stabilization' is by no means the simple thing it was light-heartedly assumed to be in the earlier years of the post-war period, and the growing intellectual preoccupation with the difficulties involved is well shown in the elaborate discussion of the problem of stabilization in the Final Report of the Gold Delegation of the League. Whilst this Report still lays it down (paragraph 193) that 'the criterion of monetary and economic policies should be their success over a period of years in maintaining the average level of wholesale prices of important international commodities relatively stable', this conclusion is hedged round with a series of qualifications and refinements which effectively dispose of the idea that an index of wholesale prices should be the sole and sufficient guide to Central Banking Policy.[2]

In the first place, an important position is assigned in the Report to short-period as well as long-period fluctuations, and the remark is made that 'we do not conceive it as possible to eliminate short-term fluctuations of the price-level', though a mitigation of the long-term fluctuations might damp down the 'cyclical' fluctuations. Secondly, the majority of the Delegation consider it 'neither possible nor desirable, by the application of

[1] Paragraph 286. (Italics not in original.)

[2] 'With reference to the other indices which should be taken as a guide to monetary policy, varying opinions, in our present state of knowledge, are likely to be held. They are all those indices which reflect business activity—the market rates of discount, the yield of bonds, the prices of different classes of shares, the value of building permits, the debits to individual deposit accounts, the production of various primary products, the international movements of capital, etc. The significance of these will vary from country to country and from epoch to epoch. No set rules for their interpretation can be laid down.' (Paragraph 196.)

monetary policy, to correct fluctuations in the price-level due to non-monetary factors' (paragraph 183). What this means is that the majority of the Delegation hold the view that (*a*) 'Some degree of cyclical oscillation is probably unavoidable, unless indeed economic society were to become almost static. Moreover, the risk must not be ignored that attempts to control fluctuations in the general or average level of prices may accumulate strains within the price-structure and therefore cause deferred and probably more violent paroxysms of readjustment eventually.' (Paragraph 134.) (*b*) 'When the decline in prices is due to improvements in industry and agriculture which have lowered production costs, the decline in prices is, on the whole, beneficial, for it is in this way that the fruits of industrial and agricultural progress are made available to society as a whole. . . . It is only when the attempt is made to sustain prices in the face of *decreasing production costs* that disequilibria occur, for this encourages over-production and causes an accumulation of goods which results ultimately in a breakdown.' (Paragraph 169.)

The maintenance of prices at a given level—as distinguished from an immediate rise in prices as a cure of the present depression—played no decisive part in the deliberations of the World Economic Conference: in view of the object with which the Conference was called together, this was not, perhaps, to be expected. The change of tone is to be gathered from Resolution 5 in the series in which the appropriate Sub-Commission of the Monetary and Financial Commission laid down the 'general principles of Central Bank monetary policy', viz: '. . . They should endeavour to adapt their measures of credit regulation, as far as their domestic position permits, to any tendency towards an undue change in the state of general business activity. An expansion of general business activity of a kind which clearly cannot be permanently maintained should lead Central Banks to introduce a bias towards credit restriction into the credit policy which they think fit to adopt, having regard to internal conditions in their own countries. On the other hand, an undue decline in general business activity in the world at large should lead them to introduce a bias towards relaxation. *In pursuing such a policy the Central Banks will have done what is in their power to reduce fluctuations in business activity and thereby also undue fluctuations in the purchasing power of gold.*'[1] In this resolution the old point of view appears to have been abandoned altogether and, what is as significant, it forms part of a wider series of statements designed to give concreteness to the 'rules of the gold standard game'. This brings me to the last of the many problems discussed in the preceding pages.

The first attempt to define the 'rules of the game', as well as the first use of the phrase itself, was made by the Macmillan Committee.[2] Recognizing the impossibility of drawing up a 'formal code of action, admitting of no exceptions and qualifications, adherence to which is obligatory on peril of wrecking the whole structure', the Report confines itself to laying down three principles. The international gold standard, firstly, involved 'a common agreement as to the ends for which it exists'. The standard, secondly, should be worked in such a way as to bring with it 'stability of prices as well as that it should guarantee stability of exchange'. Finally, 'action by individual Central Banks which, by repercussions on the policy of the others, imperils the stability of the price level should, as far as possible, be avoided'. The elaborate discussions of the Gold Delegation contain no

[1] *Reports approved by the Conference*, etc., p. 14.
[2] *Report*, paragraph 47.

formal mention of the phrase, but paragraphs 38 and 194 both incorporate what is equivalent to a code of action appropriate to a gold standard. 'Two fundamental facts', it is said in the former paragraph, 'have emerged clearly from the history of recent years and recent months—namely (i) that no international currency standard can work successfully for any protracted period if the principles on which it is conducted vary widely from one country to another; and (ii) that, whenever the general level of prices in any country important to the whole system is either out of gear with world values or insensitive to monetary influences, there is a danger of a strain being placed on the international monetary standard which it may prove unable to support.' The latter paragraph insists on the dual character of 'any policy designed to maintain the world price structure in equilibrium. . . . Those responsible for monetary policy in each country must take account both of domestic and of international considerations and these may not be easily reconcilable.' International co-operation must therefore be the device by which, it is to be hoped, national and international interests can be reconciled.

It was, however, the Monetary and Financial Commission of the World Economic Conference which attempted the most ambitious definition of the 'rules of the game' so far evolved. One of the resolutions has already been quoted above: the general tenor of the whole series can be gathered from the following summary:

1. The policy adopted by Central Banks must be such as to maintain a fundamental equilibrium. 'Gold movements which reflect a lack of such an equilibrium constitute therefore an essential factor in determining Central Bank policy.'

2. Gold sterilization and gold offsetting are condemned,

in so far as they impede gold movements which seem 'of a more permanent character'.

3. Fixed buying and selling prices of gold in the local currency must be laid down, and gold should be allowed to move freely.

4. Central Banks should be able to obtain the fullest possible information from the local money market 'concerning the demands that might be made upon their reserves'.

5. There should be continuous co-operation between Central Banks, and the Bank for International Settlements should be regarded as 'an essential agency for Central Bank action designed to harmonize conflicting views and for joint consultation'.

6. Whilst the discretion of Central Banks should not be hampered, they should recognize that, in addition to a national, they have also to fulfil a task of international character. The relation of these considerations to long-run policy is set out in the resolution quoted above.

The nature of international discussion has now been set forth: it is now necessary to turn to the future.

CHAPTER VII

THE FUTURE OF THE GOLD STANDARD: A PERSONAL INTERPRETATION

THE INTERNATIONAL gold standard has few friends to-day. The unparalleled depression of the last five years and the dangers and uncertainties of the present moment have seriously weakened its prestige and, since a large part of the world now possesses currency systems no longer linked with gold, one of its main intellectual supports has been destroyed. For one of the great justifications of the international gold standard was precisely that it *was* an international standard. So long as it existed, international trade and finance, the two great links of the world economic order, had found the monetary vehicle which most closely corresponded to their necessities; for such a standard not only allowed all prices and all debts to be expressed in a common medium: it implied, as we have seen in previous chapters, an integration of the price and income structure throughout the economic world. The ability to maintain a local currency at par with gold carried with it economic consequences of the most far-reaching kind. But every breach in the system of gold standard countries diminishes the advantages of the system. If only a single country remained upon gold, its price structure and its foreign exchange rates with the rest of the world might be more unstable than those of the remaining areas *inter se*.

There is, then, a real justification in the existing facts of the situation for regarding the international gold standard as a less useful instrument of economic progress than it once was. The facts are, however, capable of change. A resumption of gold payments by a number of countries, primarily of course by Great Britain, would at once alter the whole complexion of affairs. If the only reason for adhering to a paper standard is that the gold standard area has shrunk, that reason can disappear very speedily. But the case for refusing again to adhere to gold may be based upon much more substantial grounds; upon the inherent and intrinsic disadvantages of the gold standard itself and upon the growing degree to which rigidity and economic nationalism are preventing the gold standard, however skilfully worked, from achieving the final ends for which it was instituted.

In addition to the difficulties which have already manifested themselves in the last few years, new difficulties may emerge in the future. Were Great Britain to contemplate an immediate and independent return to the gold standard—and even if her example were to be followed by the existing 'Sterling Club', i.e. the Empire and Scandinavia—there are some very definite risks which would have to be taken into account. The world is not yet in a very settled condition and considerable doubts might be entertained as to Great Britain's ability to remain upon gold. Since a considerable volume of short term money is held in London, the Bank might again be exposed to panic runs. Again, considerable uncertainty prevails as to the future currency policy to be pursued by important countries, some of whom are in direct competition with Great Britain. Thus it is by no means certain that the U.S.A. will not be forced to make use of the powers contained in the 'Inflation Amendments' of the Agricultural Adjustment Act and to reduce the gold content of the U.S. dollar by a further 10 per cent of the old par. It is true that, if she does not do this, but, on the contrary inflates, either by the issue of 'greenbacks' or by the introduction of bimetallism or by a vast issue of silver certificates, on balance Great

Britain is likely to gain gold rather than lose it—though a flight of capital from the U.S.A. might add to that floating mass of short term balances which is the terror of all Central Bankers to-day. The point is that no one can be certain what America *will* do: and so long as uncertainty prevails, isolated action can rightly be regarded as highly venturesome. Again, even if American currency policy were less uncertain than it is, Great Britain is in direct competition, especially as regards the production of cotton textiles and artificial silk, with Japan. No guarantee can be given that, once she has committed herself to a new parity with gold, Japan will not steal a march upon her again and attempt to strengthen her hold upon the world's markets by a renewed depreciation of the yen.

If the European situation alone is taken into account, there are grounds enough for anxiety. Immediately after the failure to arrive at a provisional stabilization agreement at the World Economic Conference, the countries which have since become known as the Gold Bloc, viz, Belgium, France, Holland, Italy, Poland, and Switzerland, issued a statement to the effect that 'the undersigned governments, convinced that the maintenance of their currencies is essential for the economic and financial recovery of the world and of credit, and for the safeguarding of social progress in their respective countries, confirm their intention to maintain free functioning of the gold standard in their respective countries at the existing gold parities and within the framework of existing monetary laws. They ask their Central Banks to keep in close touch to give the maximum efficacy to this declaration.' Since that time, the members of the group have successfully withstood the American currency experiment, internal unrest (France and Holland) and national catastrophe (Poland). But no one knows what the future may hold: for the under-valuation of the paper currencies of their competitors is equivalent to an over-valuation of their own, against the effects of which, upon their tourist trade and their exports, as well as upon the prosperity of their Colonial domains, the weapon of internal price reduction is alone possible—and to that there are social as well as economic limits. It can legitimately be said that the devaluation of the Czechoslovakian crown, which occurred on February 17th 1934,[1] may be merely pointing the path which other countries may have to follow. Were Great Britain to choose a parity with gold now, might it not be the case that this parity would prove to be unsuitable if the Gold Bloc were driven to devaluation? Also, even if there were no concerted action by these countries, might it not be the case that internal pressure—from the industrialists of Belgium, the Colonial interests of Holland, the fiscal authorities in France or Poland—might lead to the break-up of the Gold Bloc with incalculable consequences on political conditions and on world finance?

If the position of the Gold Bloc can thus be represented as doubtful, the same may be said of the position in Germany. The gold standard still exists in Germany, but is it an effective standard? Her short-term debt is frozen, her long-term debt is largely subject to a moratorium, imports are hampered by far-reaching decrees, and—so far as exports are concerned—an elaborate series of regulations permits of their financing by purchases of 'blocked marks' of very numerous categories, sold at prices considerably below the nominal gold parity of the mark; without which device it is probable that the already very considerably diminished volume of German exports would shrink still further. Memories of the

[1] First announced February 11th 1934.

devastating era of inflation in Germany are still very fresh: and it may indeed be the case that even the revolutionary government which has swept away so much of the old Germany cannot risk the loss of confidence which would follow an open tampering with the standard of value: just as in France, it may be argued, the prejudices of the *rentier* and of the middle classes are more important as props of the economic order than the arguments of economists. But an autocratic Government, driven to the wall, without any organized opposition to placate, without any effective public opinion to contend with, may still venture, if the economic situation is bad enough, to run risks. Who can tell, so it can reasonably be argued, whether it will not in the end suit the book of the present National Socialist rulers of the country to devaluate the currency openly and so strengthen the competitive position of Germany?

There are two other points to be taken into account—both concerned with a problem of a different order. In recent years, there has arisen a new and unsuspected competitor for the available new supplies of gold—the private hoarder: whilst the Eastern nations, traditionally regarded as the buyers of gold for hoarding purposes, have, under the pressure of economic adversity, been disposing of their stocks, the Western capitalist, fearful of the future, has been acquiring gold as a 'store of value'. The magnitude of this private hoarding has reached astonishing figures, and the Bank for International Settlements has added to the sense of obligation due to it by drawing marked attention to the magnitude of the sums involved. In its Fourth Annual Report, after an elaborate survey of the situation, it concludes that 'through a comparison of the results obtained by different methods it may be concluded that at the beginning of 1934 it was at least 7,000 million Swiss francs, or more than two and a half times the value of the current annual gold production. The existence of this "hidden reserve", some of which will become available when confidence returns, is of great importance in connection with monetary reconstruction.'[1] But suppose confidence does not return! Even supposing that it does, there is still to be taken into account the possible effect of the diminished popularity of the gold exchange standard as an instrument of gold economy. May it not be the case that, whilst lower prices are stimulating gold discovery on the one hand, the beneficial effects which might otherwise be exerted by increased gold production on the position of the Central Banks of the world could be completely neutralized by the increased demand for gold so set up? If the world is not to be pacified, may not *both* Central Banks and Treasuries on the one hand, and the capitalist on the other, revert to the habits of an earlier age and hold gold simply because there is nothing else to be held?

Finally, it must be pointed out that the question of British indebtedness to the U.S.A. is only in abeyance; it has not yet been resolved. So long as Great Britain remains upon a paper standard, any payments to be made to the United States, however embarrassing they may be from the standpoint of budgetary equilibrium, do not involve any transfer obstacle in the shape of a rigid exchange rate, *provided that public opinion is prepared to see sterling reduced to the level appropriate to a transfer of the sums in question, however low that level may happen to be*, and provided further *that a depreciating exchange in this country does not lead to deflationary effects in other countries*. Given these conditions, the fall of the exchange

[1] *Fourth Annual Report of the B.I.S.*, p. 22. It must be added that these amounts have been hoarded over and above the very large amounts hoarded in the shape of notes, especially notes of large denominations.

necessary to effect a given volume of payments on debt acount is only a special case of the general principle that, given appropriate circumstances, a paper currency enables a country to adapt the level of its exchange rates to the level of its costs, instead of having to adapt the level of its costs to the level of the exchange, as in the case of a gold standard or, more generally, a fixed exchange.

There appears to me to be a very strong case against an independent return to the gold standard by Great Britain alone. But those who protest against such a return overlook that a refusal by Great Britain to contemplate a return to gold *at all* does not leave the general situation unchanged: that whilst it might be a good thing for Great Britain and her monetary allies to remain off gold so long as the rest of the world remained upon gold or returned to it, it by no means follows that the net results to be expected from a *general* return to gold are not superior, even from the standpoint of Great Britain, to the consequences to be expected from a continuance of the present chaos. The game of competitive exchange depreciation as a means of universal recovery, to put it frankly, is played out—the net effect has been an intensification of all those measures of mutual exclusion, which have succeeded in almost destroying international trade and in weakening the weaker raw material producing countries of the world, until they have become such bad 'risks' that it is almost impossible to lend them the sums which they need to put them on their feet again. Yet it is clear that every Commission which has investigated these matters has come to the same conclusion: that no fundamental recovery is possible without a revival of international trade, a revival of international lending, a simultaneous assault upon the monstrous Chinese walls, which greed, fear, and insecurity have created, and upon the currency conditions which have made such tariff measures appear a plausible means of defence to disinterested and public-spirited individuals. It is no argument against the position here taken up that 'nobody pays any attention to these reports': the fact that politicians are terrified to act in the way advised in the long sequence of reports analysed in the last chapter does not prove that the advice given is wrong, in the sense that if acted upon it would *not* bring about the results desired. Failure to implement these reports simply shows that, in an era of nationalism, politicians prefer to run the risk of wrecking the entire economic structure to incurring the risk of sacrificing some temporary advantage which they imagine the continuance of chaos secures to their nationals, or of being denounced by some group of opponents as 'unpatriotic'. The advice proffered and refused may still be the right advice: and the price of the refusal to pay any attention to it may simply be the continuation of the depression, with all the incalculable consequences which it entails.

Nor is it in the least true that all the dangers of an independent return to gold on the part of Great Britain would be equally present if that return were part of a concerted attempt to restore more stable currency conditions: *for some of these dangers are a function of the continuance of currency chaos, not of its removal.* It is the refusal to do anything but pay lip-service to the idea of a return to gold which has, for instance, convinced the average inhabitant of the U.S.A. that anything except a very provisional return to the gold standard would be to play into the hands of the British Equalization Exchange Fund and which has furnished the most convincing arguments to the Committee for the Nation for its anti-stabilization action and its embarrassing attacks on the

U.S.A. Government whenever it shows any signs of reasonable behaviour. The British example has encouraged the Japanese, for there is hardly an element in the British situation which does not find its parallel in the case of Japan, and, indeed, in view of the pressure of the Japanese population on the resources of a not very well endowed, limited area of land, the Japanese case for a 'free currency' is perhaps stronger than our own. If we showed signs of being really willing to stabilize in common with others, the position in the Gold Bloc countries would at once become easier, and the danger of further hoarding on the part of Continental capitalists would at once become less—thus reducing the chance that the Central Banks would be left with an inadequate supply of gold in the future. Private gold hoards are a measure of current insecurity, and an international agreement to stabilize would in all probability not only reduce the future demand of gold for private purposes, but bring out of hoard a large part of the gold already withdrawn from monetary circulation. So far from a general return to gold thus diminishing the aggregate supply of gold available for Central Banks, there is every reason to suppose that the supply would be increased.

The attitude of certain opponents of the return to gold on the part of Great Britain to the problems of the Gold Bloc countries appears to me to contain a very questionable element of thought. Their attitude appears to be that these countries 'have only themselves to blame': let them imitate the example of the paper standard countries and throw off the shackles of gold or, at any rate, let them devaluate by 30 per cent or more. If they are too stupid to do this let us do nothing until the pressure of circumstances forces such a step. Writers who argue in this way overlook the fact that the internal consequences, especially in France, of a reduction in the external value of the currency might be quite other than those in the English-speaking countries: that further, in the present era of nationalistic propaganda and practices, an addition to the number of countries attempting to secure the advantages of under-valuation would in all probability simply add to the mass of restrictive legislation which it should be the first duty of statesmen to remove. No doubt it is less offensive to the national pride of countries off gold to talk about the 'over-valuation' of the gold currencies than to speak about the under-valuation of their own; though the over-valuation of the one implies the under-valuation of the other. Provided that the existing paper standard countries are prepared to give an undertaking that, in the event of a devaluation of the Gold Bloc currencies they will not, in return, attempt to lower the external value of their currencies any further, the over-valuation of the Dutch guilder or the French franc could, of course, be cured by a fall in these currencies just as well as by a rise in the franc or guilder value of the paper currencies. If the paper standard countries are *not* prepared to give such an undertaking, they are in fact reserving for themselves the right to add to the existing chaos. If they are prepared to give such an undertaking, they are, in fact, implicitly admitting that some international regulation of the currency problem is ineluctable. The internal political risks resulting from devaluation in the gold standard countries would in any case remain.

It does not seem to me that the refusal to contemplate a return to the gold standard before prices have substantially risen is reasonable, in present world circumstances. On the contrary, I regard the refusal to return to gold as one of the major obstacles to recovery, and, therefore, to that rise of prices which is (in my opinion rightly) considered one of the conditions of economic advance—whatever qualifications may have to be introduced in view of the incessant march of technique. In the first place, one must take account of the cumulative effects upon industrial activity as well as upon the raw material producing countries of the tariff restrictions and quotas, the accentuation of which is a *direct* result of currency instability. Secondly, allowance must be made for the influence of the existing uncertainty upon enterprise and therefore upon prices. In the third place, allowance must be made for the circumstance that international loans have practically come to an end, and that this cessation of international lending not only involves continued depression in the constructional and heavy industries, which have in certain countries, especially in Great Britain, depended to a large extent upon activity in overseas countries, but also involves a continuance of that gold 'maldistribution' which is so widely deplored, as well as a continuance of the low level of primary products. If the agricultural countries of the world are to pay their debts without assistance, they must export such gold as they possess and sell their produce at such prices as they can manage to get—even if this means prices which enable them to 'jump' the tariff walls expressly set up to prevent them from doing anything of the kind. It is only if the currency arrangements of the world are such as to permit of a resumption of lending, on the one hand, and such as to rob the ultra-protectionists of their most striking arguments on the other hand, that a general world-wide rise of prices will become possible: the cause of tariff reform has become inextricably involved with the cause of currency reform.

There are two other reasons why a concerted return to the gold standard should facilitate, rather than impede, further recovery—whether recovery is defined as a rise of prices, or a resumption of industrial activity, or both these things together. It was pointed out above that one of the essentially new features of the post-war period has been the growth in the size of the International Short-Loan Fund. Now a stabilization of currencies in itself will tend to mitigate the *volatile* character of this fund: there will no longer be the same temptation or the same necessity to transfer the fund rapidly from one centre to another in order to profit from fluctuations in the relative values of currencies: relative changes in the rate of interest will no doubt continue to cause the fund, or constituent parts of it, to shift from one centre to another from time to time, but a difference of a ½ or a ¼ per cent in the rate of interest can hardly be compared to profit and loss opportunities of the magnitude permitted by the fluctuations in the relative values of currencies. Moreover, the rate of return upon short-term investments is low, and bankers are only deterred from lending 'long' by the risks involved in the present currency situation (as well as by political risks which are obviously also partly connected with the currency and tariff situation as it now is). Currency stabilization, by encouraging the revival of international lending, would at the same time encourage a reduction in the absolute size of the international short-loan fund, and thus at once stimulate a rise in prices and alleviate the technical working of the gold standard. It is, in any case, of the utmost importance to realize that the international short-loan fund problem has in recent years become not more, but less important, so far as absolute figures are concerned. The Bank for International Settlements estimates that at the end of 1930 the total volume of international short-term indebtedness amounted to 70,000 million Swiss francs—a figure which had fallen to 32,000 million Swiss francs at the end of 1933. However unwelcome the methods by which, in some cases, the reduction has been achieved, it must not be imagined that the technical problem presented by international short-term indebtedness has actually been increasing of late.[1]

Further, what is holding up price recovery is not a shortage of gold or of commerical banking reserves, but the decline in the velocity of circulation which has accompanied the depression. At the present time, the 'excess reserves' of the member banks of the Federal Reserve System are larger than they have ever been before, and the devaluation of the U.S. dollar has provided the basis for further expansion. In Great Britain 'Banker's Deposits' at the Bank of England, which, on the average of 1929, stood at £63 million, had increased almost by 50 per cent on the average of 1933 and stood at £105 millions at the end of July 1934. A revaluation of the gold stocks of the Bank on a basis approximating to the present market value of gold would add greatly to the visible banking reserve of the British Central Bank. It is not a failure of the Central Banks to provide the 'basis of credit' which is responsible for the failure of prices to rise: it is the economic situation which makes holders of bank balances unwilling to spend them. By eliminating one, and a very important, element of uncertainty, the stabilization of currencies is likely to increase velocity of circulation and therefore to stimulate a rise of prices. It is the present situation which is deflationary in its effects: not the situation which would result from stabilization, especially if it were accompanied, as it most undoubtedly would be, by the establishment of

[1] *Vide Fourth Report of the B.I.S.*, pp. 27 et seq. The whole section dealing with this subject deserves the most careful examination. The figures mentioned above include (for European countries and the U.S. only): 'financial credits and deposits with banks and similar institutions and also ordinary commercial lending.'

gold parities below those in existence before the advent of the crisis.

It is not, however, the case that a return to gold is the only alternative to the continuance of the present situation, and before arriving at a final judgment it is important to take account of the possibility of an international agreement based upon the permanent retention, in some parts of the world at least, of a paper standard. The suggestion has frequently been made that the number of countries whose currencies are linked to sterling, more or less closely, is now so great and the importance of the sterling standard is in any case so overwhelming to a large part of the world, that a permanent 'sterling club' would constitute a permanently satisfactory arrangement. Thus, it is said, it is sterling prices which are stable and gold prices which are falling: it is the sterling area which enjoys confidence and the gold area which suffers from a lack of it: it is sterling which is completely under the control of the Bank of England whilst gold is subject to the vicissitudes of nature and the panic fears of the private hoarder, as well as to the currency policy of the Central Banks of the Gold Bloc countries. Why should we not accept the 'logic of facts' and abandon once and for all the pretence that in a world dominated by nationalistic and autarchistic ideals gold can serve as a suitable basis for currency and banking arrangements?

That a world divided into two groups—one firmly and formally based upon gold, the other based upon sterling, itself kept at a fixed relationship to the gold currencies—would represent a great advance upon the present situation is indubitable, just as the present situation, in which *de facto* stabilization upon a sterling basis has become fairly general, is a great advance upon the confusion of only a short while ago.

A currency union based upon sterling, would, of course,

involve for all the areas comprehended within it, except Great Britain herself, the necessity of pursuing a currency and credit policy such that the parity with sterling, once chosen, would be maintained: otherwise the whole scheme would be an utter sham. If Great Britain desired to maintain the parity of her exchange with the gold franc or any other gold unit, she, too, would have to impose certain limitations upon her currency policy. It is, of course, quite possible to imagine certain alternatives, from Great Britain's standpoint. Instead of maintaining *de facto* stability of the pound with gold, she might choose to pursue a 'managed currency' policy, in the sense of attempting to keep general prices or wholseale prices or the cost of living index constant in terms of pounds. Or, lastly, Great Britain might refuse to avow any fixed objective whatsoever, and simply pursue, from time to time, such objectives as seemed best under actual circumstances. In all cases, except the last, however, Great Britain's freedom of action would be circumscribed, just as much as if she were back upon the gold standard and in *all* cases, even the last one, the independence of action of all the other members would be limited in exactly the same way as if they (and Great Britain as well) were back upon gold. From their point of view it makes no difference whether the pound is a certain weight of gold or not, so long as their local unit of account is to be kept equal to a certain fixed number of pounds. It might be said that if the purchasing price of the pound rises or remains steady, it would be technically easier to maintain parity with it, than it would be with gold: but obviously this depends upon the assumption that the purchasing power of gold will rise in the future and that technical efficiency will not keep pace with the fall in prices. The argument also assumes that the level of sterling prices is the dominant consideration in maintaining parity between the various currencies comprehended in the proposed union. It might very well be the case, however, that the type of economic policy of which a managed currency is the expression in the monetary sphere involves measures which, in other respects, are harmful to economic interests outside Great Britain. It might be better to support a return to gold, even though this meant prices falling somewhat faster than efficiency, provided it meant *also* a freeing of the capital markets and a return to relatively freer trade conditions, than to support a managed currency policy, so long as this was an integral part of a policy of economic exclusiveness. So long as Great Britain continues to be the important market for all agricultural and raw material producers that she is now, a large part of the world must necessarily subordinate local currency policy to the course of sterling—at least in the sense that local currencies must not cost so much in terms of sterling that the British market becomes closed to the local producers. But this situation may alter if Great Britain turns her back, as far as she can, upon overseas suppliers. In any case, it means that the 'sterling Club' is liable to internal stresses and strains. For the temptation will be to force the value of the local currency down in order to retain the British market: on the other hand, it means that British policy becomes a factor of too great significance in the maintenance of the Sterling Group. Communities may be prepared to accord to 'natural vicissitude' a certain degree of willing subordination; but if the local difficulties can be ascribed plausibly to the policy pursued by another country, there will be a temptation to take one's fate into one's own hands. The Sterling Group, just because it is based on sterling, will be an unstable organization—unless we can imagine the affairs of the group managed in common: but that would greatly diminish the attractiveness of the proposal to Great Britain. The temptation to Great Britain to pursue the policy which she thinks best suited to her needs without overmuch reference to the wishes of her partners is very great: she can get on without them at present to a greater extent than they can do without her. The Sterling Group is a polite expression for British monetary hegemony: its attractiveness will depend upon how far the other members of the group will tolerate this predominance indefinitely and on the wisdom or unwisdom with which British monetary affairs are conducted in the future as well as in the present. This brings me back to the central difficulties of any system of managed currency: *it has to be managed,* and it is possible to doubt both the objectives and the managers. The result is that it is not easy to maintain permanently a halfway house arrangement between local autonomy and the return to gold. If the world is to 'plan' its currency arrangements it will prefer local management and the risk of local differences of policy: if there is to be subordination it had better be upon a basis which limits the degree of discretion (perhaps one ought to say indiscretion) involved in the management of the currency standard.

The danger that a managed currency will sooner or later be abused has always been one of the props of the gold standard. Further, the concept of a managed standard as a permanent institution is still strange and unwelcome to a large part of the business world and of the public generally. Public opinion is coloured to a far greater degree than many economists in this country are prepared to admit by historical and therefore, from some points of view, irrational preferences. The suspension of the gold standard, even in areas where it has been a not infrequent occurrence, e.g. in South America, has not been regarded as a step towards a better state of affairs, but as an unwelcome consequence of a state of grave and unusual pressure. The gold standard has certain psychological supports behind it the value of which must not be underestimated. Moreover, the short-run objective which the managers of the gold standard have to keep before their eyes is simple and intelligible, and experience shows that it is one which is capable of being attained even without the aid of elaborate machinery. What, then, explains the undoubted popularity of alternative currency systems at the present time?

Firstly, just as the restored gold standard of 1924–29 acquired a certain measure of popularity because its restoration coincided with a very considerable degree of economic prosperity in the majority of countries, so it has suffered in the last few years because its continuance coincided with widespread depression. Secondly, the fact that in the majority of countries the standard was abandoned and that complete confusion did not ensue strengthens the conviction that at best the gold standard was only a 'fair-weather' standard and the alternatives were not as black as they were usually painted: the fact has been overlooked that fluctuating currencies were used as a defence for a policy of economic isolation, and economic isolation was then used as a defence for fluctuating currencies—with the result that world trade has been largely destroyed. But the main reason for the popularity of alternatives to the gold standard, lies, I think, elsewhere. Wide circles have accepted the ideas that (1) the objective of monetary policy should be the stabilization of prices; (2) the stabilization of prices is not consistent with the gold standard, which should therefore be rejected; (3) economic science sanctions these views, so that a return to gold would be against the weight of 'scientific' authority in these matters.

It goes without saying that economists of great standing and authority are among those who believe that a stabilization of the price level is the proper objective of monetary policy and that this objective, to be successfully attained, requires the abandonment of gold. It is also the case that—as was seen in the last chapter—the idea of stabilization of prices, for a time at least, perhaps represented the view of the majority of those called upon to advise governments in these matters. It would be wrong, however, to pretend that to-day the bulk of responsible economic opinion in this country would still be prepared to adhere to a policy of price stabilization, or that it would be prepared to reject the gold standard, if the impossibility of stabilizing prices were the sole ground of hesitation. From a relatively early date in the discussion of these problems British economists, for example the Macmillan Committee, have emphasized that a fall of prices which did no more than register the advance of technique was no obstacle to the smooth working of the economic system. More recently experience has shown in the case of the U.S.A. that relatively stable prices are not a protection against boom conditions, whilst an analytical explanation of why price stabilization in the U.S.A. before the break of 1929 actually made things worse has also been forthcoming. To prevent prices from falling, if improvements in production tend to push them down, is to add to the inflationary elements always present in a boom period and therefore to aggravate both the boom itself and the subsequent depression.

It is no longer the stabilization of prices, but increased stability in general which now attracts economists as constituting the true aim of monetary policy. Whether stability be defined as an attempt to maximize over time the regularity of the national or the world income, or whether it be defined as maximizing the volume of employment, or simply defined as an attempt to 'damp down' the amplitude of the trade cycle, is of greater scientific than of practical importance. All these definitions are consistent with one another. Moreover, whilst any attempt to stabilize the long-period trend of prices would be abandoned, stability in the above sense is quite consistent with a diminution in the violence of price fluctuations in the short-run, and it is these which have proved so disastrous to business in the past.

In so far as the case against the gold standard rests upon the superior ease with which prices can be maintained stable over time with a paper standard in being, it must be abandoned as soon as long-period stabilization is no longer regarded as the major objective. If *this* is to be the reason for preferring paper, the substitution of another objective is all that is necessary to raise the status of the gold standard again: and the rejection of the principle of price stabilization in fact substantially alters the position, positively and not merely negatively. For once this objective is abandoned, a whole series of difficulties connected with the working of the gold standard also disappears. *The pursuit of stability is just as much part of the traditional task of Central Banks as the maintenance of parity of the exchange and is perfectly consistent with this second objective.* By restoring stability as the objective, in place of price stabilization, we postulate aims familiar to Central Bankers for decades: we bid them pursue an end for which the machinery at their command is adequate: which, finally, if attained, will satisfy the world's needs better than the ideal for which it has been substituted. The sufferings and agonies of the last five years are the result of neglecting trade cycle factors and watching only price factors. Before the depression began the slogan was 'watch the price level and let the trade cycle look after itself': in fact, there were not wanting voices which urged that, given the elimination of price fluctuations, the trade cycle would automatically disappear. Attention was concentrated, not upon the imperfections of the end, but upon the imperfections of the means. There is no need to repeat this mistake, in the light of the experiences of the recent past. The gold standard is perfectly consistent with later developments of thought: and those later developments are only the consequence of a realization that the ideal of price stabilization has broken down as the standard by which the conduct of Central Banks should be measured.

It does not follow, of course, that a price level falling faster over time than the growth of technical efficiency warrants has not grave disadvantages, in an age in which contractual obligations (since they now comprehend social service payments of many kinds) are more significant than they have ever been before. Nor does it follow that it is inadvisable or illegitimate to make use of such measures of alleviation, for example, economy of gold reserves, as are available. All that is urged here is that measures intended to correct such evils are of less importance than policies designed to prevent violent short-period fluctuations in industrial and economic activity generally—these being the fluctuations which induce the violent short-period fluctuations in *prices* of which we have been witnesses recently. As a subordinate end of monetary policy, we may hope to influence the long-period trend: but any measures that we take should not assume the form of preventing the natural consequences of increasing abundance and improved technique.

To show that a return to gold is desirable is not, of course, by any means the same thing as proving that public opinion is ripe for the change, or that the interested governments are prepared to make any decisive move in this direction: governments can plead that they cannot move before opinion is ripe, and opinion refuses to ripen because governments hesitate to act. It also remains true that the continuance, to a greater or lesser degree in different countries, of widespread unemployment, of refusal to invest and to venture savings, is a sign that prices and costs have not been brought into equilibrium in all directions and if recovery in all directions is to be made the prior condition for action, refusal to act is at present justified. All that can be urged is that recovery would be greater if action were initiated, and that if nothing positive is to be done before all 'disturbing' factors are out of the way, nothing will ever be done at all. The vicious circle can only be broken if it is realized that the initiation of action can be separated by an interval of time from the final completion of policy. 'All experience points to the desirability of some, perhaps considerable, interval of time between *de facto* and *de jure* stabilization. Thus the issue before us is one of taking decisions which will govern policy, rather than of formulating laws which determine the technical character of the currency systems of the world.

'It is much more important that the determination of the States of the world to proceed to an effective regulation of their currencies should be made manifest than that, at this particular juncture of events, a rigid time-table should be drawn up. The important points to be taken into account seem to be the following:

> '(i) The announcement, in such a form as to carry conviction, of the intention to proceed to a *de jure* stabilization:

'(ii) The determination of the conditions under which it should be considered safe to return to the gold standard.

'(iii) The creation of the appropriate machinery to review the situation and to formulate plans.'

So I wrote in the early spring of 1934,[1] and I see no reason to alter now the views which I expressed then. The most urgent task of the moment is to formulate a practical policy which takes account of legitimate apprehensions and susceptibilities. In what follows—based upon the Memorandum cited below—I make the attempt to round off this discussion of the problems of the gold standard by providing what I believe to be a policy suitable to the circumstances of the present time.

It is impossible to imagine a return to gold without some kind of organized international discussion and for this purpose a new Monetary Conference must be called, composed of at least the leading economic and financial States of the world. It must be called for no other purpose than to consider monetary reform and, if it is to do its work successfully, its membership must be limited. I am of the opinion that if the U.S.A., Great Britain, Japan, France, and Germany composed the Conference membership, that would be all that is necessary: though, naturally, the members of the 'Sterling Club' have an interest in the question of whether the pound goes back to a gold basis or not, that interest appears to me to be a *mediate* one: their immediate interest concerns the rate of exchange between sterling and their own local currency and that is not an issue which is directly affected by the question of whether the pound is a gold pound or a paper pound. The five

[1] 'Memorandum on Monetary Policy, submitted to the Monetary Committee of the International Chambers of Commerce.' (*World Trade*, April 1934.)

countries mentioned represent between them the four types of currency standard characteristic of the present time: (1) the orthodox gold standard; (2) the provisional gold standard; (3) the gold standard subject to drastic exchange controls; (4) the free paper standard, buttressed by an exchange equalization fund. Agreement between these countries would inevitably lead to such a strengthening of the prestige of the gold standard that, whether everywhere at once re-adopted or not, the trend would henceforth be in that direction rather than away from it, as has been the case ever since the abandonment of gold by Great Britain. The principles which underlie any attempt at re-stabilization are simple.

(1) One may take it as axiomatic that none of the countries at present off gold is likely to want to go back without the others going back simultaneously. It would, I think, be unreasonable to expect Great Britain to go back without knowing the intentions of Japan, and the present policy of the U.S.A. is, after all, only provisional. (2) The object should be to fix the new gold content of all the unstabilized currencies. The danger is that the proposed Conference will degenerate into a mere wrangle over the new parities. I suggest that the object should be to persuade the U.S.A. to agree not to use the President's discretionary power to lower the dollar to 50 cents gold provided that Great Britain agrees to the present dollar/sterling and sterling/yen rates, and provided that the Gold Bloc does not devaluate, or, if devaluation is decided upon, it shall only be within limits agreed upon by all signatories. (3) *De jure* stabilization should be recognized as lying some time ahead—it ought to be laid down that the rates fixed should be maintained for at least two years before *de jure* stabilization is attempted. Such *de jure* stabilization should take place simultaneously, if and when it takes place. (4) The fact should

be frankly faced that certain currencies are at present undervalued and that this undervaluation will give such countries a temporary export advantage until internal price levels have become adjusted. If this undoubted fact is to be used as an argument for a new series of exchange depreciations on the part of other countries, no agreement will ever be reached, for there will then follow, in all probability, a new series of retaliatory measures. It follows from this that the proposed Conference should lay down the principle that, *de facto* stabilization on the basis of the new gold prices having been attained, a significant alteration in the exchange rates of any one of the signatory countries should only be permitted with the consent of the others, on grounds which are capable of scientific statement and justification. It *may* prove to be the case that, in the era of provisional stabilization, a particular country finds that it can with difficulty maintain the rate at which its currency is temporarily stabilized. I see no reason why it should not be recognized that in such a case, if a convincing demonstration of the difficulties involved is furnished, the country in question should be able to obtain the consent of the others to a revision of its rate.

The great point to aim at is to prevent the renewal of chaos in the foreign exchanges and the only way of avoiding it is international co-operation in the sphere of currency reform. Perhaps, if this programme appears too ambitious, the proposed Conference might confine itself to two points

(1) the re-affirmation of the intention of the contracting parties to return to gold;

(2) the expression of a willingness of the contracting parties not to allow their exchange rates to vary by more than a certain percentage, i.e. the universalization of the American right to vary the

gold value of the dollar between 60 and 50 cents gold. In these circumstances, there would be three stages: (*a*) fluctuating within previously defined limits; (*b*) *de facto* stabilization; (*c*) *de jure* stabilization. In the last twelve months we have had tangible demonstration of the congruity of a considerable degree of recovery with relative stability and it would be disastrous to revert to a (relatively) less stable position than the one already attained.

There is, however, another series of problems of a different character—the future of the various systems of exchange control. A real recovery of international trade is not consistent with these restrictions, since, in effect, exchange control systems are perhaps the most insidious form of extreme protectionism which the world has ever seen. Something must be done about them and the following procedure is suggested:

(1) Granted that the countries which have practised exchange depreciation are prepared to abandon any further resort to this device, the countries which practise exchange control should be prepared to liberate new international transactions from any control whatsoever. This is the policy of the 'clean cut' between old and new international trade arrangements.

(2) So far as the old transactions are concerned, these countries should be prepared to agree to one or other of the two following alternatives: (*a*) to 'decontrol' all past transactions provided that the other countries (those utilizing exchange depreciation) are prepared to admit a certain devaluation of the currencies in question, e.g. to see the Austrian crown or the German mark quoted at a new parity; (*b*) to continue 'controls' provided that the existing

official rates be maintained, whilst effective arrangements are made (where they do not already exist) by which old outstanding accounts are effectively liquidated.

These proposed arrangements are based on the assumption that the restoration of international trade and of international lending are dependent upon the restoration of fixed exchange rates and of a free exchange market. If this fundamental assumption is denied, or if the restoration of increased international lending and trade is declared to be without significance to world recovery, the weight of the argument is naturally diminished. But I do not think it will be disputed that it is impossible to restore the pre-depression level of welfare without a restoration of world trade and investment to something like the level of 1929.

STATISTICAL APPENDIX

TABLE I

U.K. PRICES

(1914=100)

	Cost of Living Index		Wholesale Price Index
	All Items	Food.	
1928 Average . .	166	157	140·3
1929 Average . .	164	154	136·5
1930 Average . .	158	145	119·5
1931 Average . .	147½	131	111·7
1932 Average . .	144	126	101·6
1933 Jan. 1st . .	142	123	100·3
Feb. 1st . .	141	122	98·9
March 1st .	139	119	97·6
April 1st. .	137	115	97·2
May 1st . .	136	114	99·2
June 1st. .	136	114	101·7
July 1st . .	138	118	102·3
Aug. 1st . .	139	119	102·5
Sept. 1st. .	141	122	103·0
Oct. 1st . .	141	123	102·6
Nov. 1st . .	143	126	102.8
Dec. 1st . .	143	126	102·8
1934 Jan. 1st . .	142	124	104·6
Feb. 1st . .	141	122	105·3
March 1st .	140	120	103·8
April 1st .	139	118	102·8
May 1st . .	137	116	102·4
June 1st . .	138	117	103·6
July 1st . .	141	121	103·4

TABLE II

U.S.A. PRICES

(1913=100)

	General Price Level.*	Wholesale Price Index†
1928 Average . .	176	138·6
1929 Average . .	179	136·5
1930 Average . .	168	123·8
1931 Average . .	150	104·6
1932 Average . .	132	91·7
1933 Jan. . .	127	86·2
Feb. . .	124	84·5
March . .	123	85·1
April . .	124	85·4
May . .	127	88·6
June . .	128	91·9
July . .	132	97·5
August . .	132	98·4
Sept. . .	133	101·5
Oct. . .	133	102·0
Nov. . .	133	102·0
Dec. . .	132	101·5
1934 Jan. . .	133	103·5
Feb. . .	136	105·5
March . .	136	105·6
April . .	137	105§
May . .	136	106§
June . .	137‡	

* From *Monthly Bulletin, Federal Reserve Bank of New York.*

† From *Monthly Labour Review, U.S.A.*, May 1934, adjusted to 1913 as base.

‡ Preliminary Figure.

§ From *Federal Reserve Bulletin,* July 1934.

TABLE III

AMERICAN AND BRITISH LOANS TO OVERSEAS AREAS

	U.S.A.* $ Millions		U.K.† £ Millions
1928 . . .	1251		143
1929 . . .	671		94
1930 . . .	905		109
1931 . .	229		46
1932 . . .	8		29
1933 Jan.	0	7	12
Feb.	0		
March	0		
April	0		
May	0		
June	7		
July	5	5	26
August	0		
Sept.	0		
Oct.	0		
Nov.	0		
Dec.	0		
1934 Jan.	0	0	22
Feb.	0		
March	0		
April	0		
May	0		
June	0		

* From *Federal Reserve Bulletin*.

† From *Midland Bank Monthly Review*, June–July, 1931, Dec., 1933–Jan. 1934, and June–July, 1934.

TABLE IV

CAPITAL ISSUES IN PRINCIPAL COUNTRIES*

(000,000's omitted)

Period	United Kingdom	Austria	Czechoslovakia	France	Germany	Italy	Netherlands
Monthly Average	£	Schillings	Koruna	Francs	Marks	Lire	Gulden
1913 .	16·3	—	—	—	60	23	13
1928 .	30·8	12·0	60	876	110·0	450	50
1929 .	23·3	8·6	55	1259	80·2	607	29
1930 .	22·3	4·8	38	1832	46·6	514	45
1931 .	8·5	3·1	42	1362	65·2	361	20
1932 .	15·7	4·9	27	511	12·3	304	31
1933 .	20·4	17·9	21	300	7·3	—	—
1934 .							
Jan. .	8·5	3·3	9	95	10·2	83	6
Feb. .	7·7	20·6	—	946	18·1	—	—
March	4·0	0·1	—	34	5·9	—	—
April .	49·5	5·5	—	1206	5·1	—	—
May .	19·7	5·0	—	286	—	—	—

Period	Poland	Rumania	Sweden	Switzerland	British India	Japan	U.S.A.
Monthly Average	Zloty	Lei	Kronor	Francs	Rupees	Yen	Dollars
1913 .	—	20	18	44	56	45	—
1928 .	27·1	384	31	57	24	335	676
1929 .	17·8	318	23	81	56	222	849
1930 .	17·5	460	21	125	24	205	587
1931 .	6·4	210	28	109	27	261	259
1932 .	11·6	37	11	80	33	—	99
1933 .	3·0	47	8	15	—	551	60
1934 .							
Jan. .	0·8	158	7	38	21	297	48
Feb. .	9·3	181	8	—	—	—	—
March	0·6	28	8	—	—	—	75
April .	—	—	5·0	—	—	—	143
May .	—	—	10·6	—	—	—	—

* From *The Economist*

TABLE V

U.S.A. BALANCE OF PAYMENTS*

(Millions of dollars)

Transactions	1928	1929	1930	1931	1932†	1933
I. Current Items:						
Due to U.S.A. on account of—						
(1) Merchandise Surplus . .	1,037	841	782	334	289	22
(2) Interest on Investments .	534	565	616	536	393	36
(3) War Debts	207	207	241	113	99	2
Total	1,778	1,613	1,639	983	781	61
Due to Foreign Countries by U.S.A. .						
(1) Shipping Services	80	66	96	72	45	1
(2) Tourist Expenditure . . .	552	638	602	456	375	22
(3) Immigrant Remittances. . .	276	265	215	202	163	13
(4) Governmental & Miscell. Expenditure	145	197	97	93	67	5
Balance due to U.S.A.	725	447	629	160	131	19
II. Capital Movements:						
(1) Currency Notes exported or returned to U.S.A.	40	15	−20‡	10	80	9
(2) Gold Shipments	−272§	120	278	−176§	11	−23
(3) Short-term Credits made by U.S.A. .	188	80	485	709	409	41
(4) Long-term Loans made by U.S.A. .	675	141	278	−218¶	−217¶	−13
Total	631	356	1,021	325	283	14
Balance representing errors and omissions .	94	91	−392	−165	−152	5

* From *The Economist*, April 14th 1933. (Based on figures of the U.S. Dept. of Comm
† Provisional ‡ Export of notes from U.S.A. § Gold exports from U
¶ Purchase of U.S. securities by foreigners.

TABLE VI

FEDERAL RESERVE HOLDINGS OF BILLS AND DEPOSITS ON ACCOUNT OF FOREIGNERS*

(Thousands of dollars)

End of		Foreign Bank Deposits	Contingent Liability on Bills purchased for Foreign Correspondents
1928	June	9,066	307,714
	Dec.	5,775	324,699
1929	June	6,273	422,834
	Dec.	5,710	547,962
1930	June	5,879	469,675
	Dec.	5,761	439,288
1931	June	33,912	340,845
	Dec.	79,099	250,621
1932	June	9,002	97,729
	Dec.	19,446	40,170
1933	Jan.	40,003	40,914
	Feb.	40,125	29,984
	March	16,384	45,305
	April	29,928	40,060
	May	7,848	35,731
	June	15,523	35,854
	July	19,023	37,120
	August	37,376	40,176
	Sept.	13,504	41,462
	Oct.	16,186	31,294
	Nov.	5,324	2,893
	Dec.	4,233	3,810
1934	Jan.	3,952	4,477
	Feb.	3,433	4,835
	March	5,941	4,937
	April	6,228	4,296
	May	3,743	2,672
	June	4,893	1,524

* *From Federal Reserve Bulletin.*

TABLE VII

U.K. BALANCE OF PAYMENTS ON INCOME ACCOUNT, 1925–1933

	1925	1926	1927	1928	1929	1930	1931	1932
Excess of imports of merchandise and bullion . . .	384	475	390	358	381	386	408	287
Estimated excess of Government payments made overseas	11	—	—	—	—	—	—	24
	395	475	390	358	381	386	408	311
Estimated excess of Government receipts from overseas .	—	4	1	15	24	19	14	—
Estimated net national shipping income . . .	124	120	140	130	130	105	80	70
Estimated net income from overseas investments . . .	250	285	285	270	250	220	170	145
Estimated net receipts from short interest and commissions	60	60	63	65	65	55	30	25
Estimated net receipts from other sources . . .	15	15	15	15	15	15	10	15
Total	449	484	504	495	484	414	304	255
Estimated total credit balance on items specified above .	+54	+9	+114	+137	+103	+28	−104	−56

* *No appreciable excess of payments over receipts.*

TABLE VIII

AVERAGE BANK OF ENGLAND GOLD STOCK AND MONTH TO MONTH CHANGE

Averages of Wednesday Figures	1931	1932	1933	1934	Month to Month Change			
					1931	1932	1933	1934
January . .	143·0	120·8	120·7	190·8	− 7·5	—	− 8·9	+ 0·
February . .	140·5	120·8	132·0	190·9	− 2·5	—	+ 11·3	+ 0·
March . . .	141·9	120·8	163·6	191·0	+ 1·4	—	+ 31·6	+ 0·
April . . .	145·6	120·8	181·2	191·1	+ 3·7	—	+ 17·6	+ 0·
May . . .	149·4	122·4	186·1	191·3	+ 3·8	+ 1·6	+ 4·9	+ 0·
June . . .	157·7	133·3	187·8	191·4	+ 8·3	+ 10·9	+ 1·7	+ 0·
July . . .	154·5	136·7	189·8	—	− 3·2	+ 3·4	+ 2·0	—
August . .	133·1	138·7	190·2	—	− 21·4	+ 2·0	+ 0·4	—
September . .	134·9	139·3	190·4	—	+ 1·8	+ 0·6	+ 0·2	—
October . .	135·5	139·4	190·4	—	+ 0·6	+ 0·1	—	—
November . .	120·7	139·4	190·5	—	− 14·8	—	+ 0·1	—
December . .	120·7	129·6	190·7	—	—	− 9·8	+ 0·2	—

TABLE

GOLD RESERVES* OF CENTRAL

(Millions of

Date	North America		Europe					
	U.S.A.	Canada	Austria	Belgium	Bulgaria	Czecho-slovakia	Denmark	England
1928 June† .	3,732	104	16	110	9	30	49	826
Dec. .	3·746	114	24	126	10	34	46	748
1929 June .	3,956	76	24	139	10	34	46	774
Dec. .	3,900	78	24	163	10	37	46	710
1930 June .	4,178	81	24	167	10	39	46	763
Dec. .	4,225	110	30	191	10	46	46	718
1931 June .	4,593	87	30	199	11	46	46	793
Dec. .	4,051	78	27	354	11	49	39	588
1932 June .	3,466	78	21	357	11	49	36	663
Dec. .	4,045	84	21	361	11	51	36	583
1933 Jan. .	4,074	84	21	362	11	51	36	602
Feb. .	3,808	84	21	366	11	51	36	692
March .	3,916	81	21	371	11	51	36	836
April .	3,997	77	21	371	11	51	36	905
May .	3,991	77	21	371	11	51	36	907
June .	3,997	77	21	372	11	51	36	922
July .	4,001	77	21	374	11	51	36	925
Aug. .	4,009	77	21	375	11	51	36	926
Sept. .	4,011	77	24	376	11	51	36	926
Oct. .	4,011	77	24	377	11	51	36	927
Nov. .	4,012	77	24	378	11	51	36	928
Dec. .	4,012	77	27	380	11	51	36	928
1934 Jan. .	4,033	77	27	382	11	51	36	929
1934 Jan.‡§ .	6,829	130	45	646	19	86	60	1,573
Feb. .	7,438	130	45	639	19	112	60	1,574
March .	7,694	130	45	635	19	111	60	1,574

* From *The Federal Reserve Bulletin.*

† $1 = 25$\frac{8}{10}$ grains of gold $\frac{9}{10}$ fine: i.e. an ounce of gold = $20·67.

‡ Figures given in terms of new parity for purposes of comparison only; new parity did not become effective until after close of business, January 31st 1934.

§ $1 = 15$\frac{5}{21}$ grains of gold $\frac{9}{10}$ fine: i.e. an ounce of gold = $35.

dollars)

Europe (*continued*)										
France	Germany	Greece	Hungary	Italy	Netherlands	Norway	Poland	Portugal	Rumania	Spain
1,136	496	7	34	259	175	39	67	9	51	503
1,254	650	7	35	266	175	39	70	9	49	494
1,436	455	8	31	271	176	39	70	9	52	494
1,633	544	8	28	273	180	39	79	9	55	495
1,727	624	8	28	274	174	39	79	9	56	477
2,100	528	7	28	279	171	39	63	9	56	471
2,212	339	6	20	282	200	39	64	11	53	469
2,699	234	11	18	296	357	41	67	13	58	434
3,218	198	7	17	298	394	40	54	17	57	435
3,254	192	8	17	307	415	39	56	24	57	436
3,221	196	7	17	308	413	39	57	25	57	436
3,176	183	8	17	325	410	39	58	27	57	436
3,152	176	9	17	331	381	40	55	30	58	438
3,170	98	11	17	343	374	40	55	30	58	436
3,173	89	13	17	352	336	40	53	31	58	436
3,185	45	14	17	356	309	40	53	31	58	436
3,213	58	17	17	368	311	40	53	32	58	436
3,223	73	19	17	370	332	39	53	32	59	436
3,218	87	21	17	371	338	41	53	32	59	436
3,176	94	21	17	371	359	40	53	32	59	436
3,051	97	23	14	373	370	40	53	33	59	436
3,022	92	24	14	373	371	38	53	34	59	436
3,021	90	22	14	373	370	38	54	34	60	436
5,109	152	37	23	633	626	64	91	58	100	739
4,904	134	38	23	633	539	61	91	62	101	739
4,947	96	39	23	613	535	61	91	65	101	739

TABLE

GOLD RESERVES* OF CENTRAL

(Millions

Date		Europe (*continued*)				Latin America		
		Sweden	Switzer-land	U.S.S.R.	Yugo-slavia	Argentine	Chile	Colombia
1928	June†	62	86	80	17	622	7	23
	Dec.	63	103	92	18	607	7	24
1929	June	63	96	93	18	525	8	25
	Dec.	66	115	147	18	434	8	22
1930	June	65	112	203	19	440	8	20
	Dec.	65	138	249	19	412	7	17
1931	June	64	162	262	27	350	8	10
	Dec.	55	453	328	31	253	12	9
1932	June	55	503	349	31	249	12	13
	Dec.	55	477	368	31	249	10	12
1933	Jan.	55	477	368	31	249	10	12
	Feb.	55	488	368	31	249	10	13
	March	62	489	368	31	249	11	13
	April	71	460	368	31	249	11	14
	May	71	397	368	32	249	11	14
	June	71	361	401	32	249	11	15
	July	91	351	401	32	249	11	15
	Aug.	97	351	401	32	249	11	15
	Sept.	101	356	416	32	249	11	15
	Oct.	101	373	416	32	249	11	15
	Nov.	99	386	416	32	244	11	15
	Dec.	99	386	416	32	239	12	14
1934	Jan.	100	386	416	32	239	12	14
1934	Jan.‡§	169	653	704	53	405	20	24
	Feb.	169	600	704	53	405	20	24
	March	170	570	706	53	405	20	25

(See footnotes on p. 180.)

IX—(*continued*)

BANKS AND GOVERNMENTS

of dollars)

Latin America (*continued*)			Asia and Oceania							Africa	
Mexico	Peru	Uruguay	Australia	India	Japan	Java	New Zealand	Siam	Turkey	Egypt	S. Africa
8	21	68	111	119	541	70	36	—	—	19	40
6	22	68	109	124	541	68	35	—	—	18	39
4	22	68	108	128	542	65	35	—	—	18	38
7	22	68	90	128	542	56	32	—	—	19	36
6	17	64	98	128	434	56	33	—	—	19	34
4	18	60	75	128	412	56	33	—	—	20	33
5	16	58	75	151	425	46	34	—	—	21	31
3	17	53	52	162	234	45	32	23	—	21	39
1	11	50	52	162	214	42	30	28	9	33	38
4	11	48	42	162	212	42	25	28	10	33	35
5	11	49	42	162	212	42	25	28	10	33	38
6	11	50	42	162	212	45	25	28	10	33	50
9	11	49	21	162	212	45	25	28	10	33	54
12	11	50	4	162	212	43	25	28	10	33	52
19	11	50	3	162	212	43	25	0	10	33	65
24	11	50	3	162	212	42	25	0	11	33	70
21	11	50	3	162	212	40	25	0	11	33	80
20	11	50	3	162	212	40	25	0	11	33	75
26	11	50	3	162	212	39	24	0	11	33	72
23	11	49	3	162	212	40	25	0	11	33	80
20	11	50	4	162	212	42	25	0	11	33	82
21	11	50	3	162	212	44	24	0	12	33	83
21	11	51	3	162	212	45	25	0	12	33	84
36	19	86	6	274	359	76	42	0	20	56	143
29	20	87	6	274	359	79	42	0	20	55	150
34	19	87	5	274	359	77	42	0	20	55	146

TABLE X

GOLD PRODUCTION, 1915, 1929-33*

Year.	Union of South Africa.	U.S.A.	Canada.	Other Producing Countries.	Total for World.	
	Thousands of Ounces of Fine Gold.					Millions of Swiss francs
1915 .	9,096	4,888	918	7,692	22,594	2,420
1929 .	10,412	2,208	1,928	5,037	19,585	2,098
1930 .	10,716	2,286	2,102	5,646	20,750	2,223
1931 .	10,878	2,396	2,694	6,238	22,206	2,379
1932 .	11,559	2,449	3,044	7,174	24,226	2,595
1933 .	11,012	2,537	2,938	8,233	24,720	2,648

* *Fourth Annual Report of the Bank for International Settlements*, p. 18.

Jarrold & Sons, Limited, The Empire Press, Norwich

For Product Safety Concerns and Information please contact our EU representative GPSR@taylorandfrancis.com Taylor & Francis Verlag GmbH, Kaufingerstraße 24, 80331 München, Germany